HAL LEONARD GUITAR METHOD

Supplement to Any Guitar Method

FINGERSTYLE GUITAR

BY CHAD JOHNSON

TRACK

ISBN 978-0-634-09995-3

HAL•LEONARD®
CORPORATION

7777 W. BLUEMOUND RD. P.O. BOX 13819 MILWAUKEE, WI 53213

Visit Hal Leonard Online at
www.halleonard.com

INTRODUCTION

Welcome to the *Hal Leonard Fingerstyle Guitar Method*. This book supplements the concepts and techniques taught in the basic *Hal Leonard Guitar Method*, only it's focused on fingerstyle techniques, as they apply to the steel-string acoustic guitar. Specifically, *Fingerstyle Guitar* is aimed at the intermediate-level player who is comfortable using a pick but has little or no experience with fingerstyle techniques. Though the book starts with the basics of fingerstyle guitar, which means some of the early material may be nothing more than a review to the more experienced fingerstyle players, it builds upon previous concepts throughout. Therefore, you should play through this book from beginning to end for best results.

One of the most exciting aspects of *Fingerstyle Guitar* is that, while some elementary examples are included to demonstrate certain techniques, many others are excerpts from real songs by such fingerstyle guitar legends as Leo Kottke, Adrian Legg, David Wilcox, and James Taylor. These examples demonstrate how the many concepts covered in this book can be applied in real-world musical situations. What better way to learn than from the masters themselves?

ABOUT THE AUDIO 🔊

The accompanying CD contains audio demonstrations of many examples in this book. The corresponding track number for each song or example is listed below the audio icon.

Guitar: Doug Boduch
Recorded, mixed, and mastered by Doug Boduch

CHOOSING AN ACOUSTIC GUITAR

When purchasing your first acoustic guitar, you're likely to be overwhelmed by the endless choices available today. Virtually every aspect of the guitar will affect its tone, including the type of wood, presence of a cutaway, type of bracing, and even the finish. The intent of this section is to provide some guidelines that will hopefully make the task of choosing the right equipment a bit easier.

Guitars, like most musical instruments, are very personal objects. Players often develop a strong attachment to their instrument when they find one that feels right to them. No two players' hands or arms are exactly alike, and the feel of a guitar is equally important as the sound or look. You may have your heart set on buying the guitar used by your favorite player. If, however, you discover that guitar just doesn't feel right to you, you'd be better off continuing your search rather than forcing the instrument onto yourself. Remember, you're going to be spending (hopefully) a lot of time on the instrument, and the last thing you need is the frustration of playing an instrument that fights rather than facilitates your desire to make music. With the myriad options available, you're sure to find the sound, look, *and* feel that's right for you, if you're willing to shop around a bit.

SIZE AND TYPE

Within the realm of the acoustic guitar, there are many different types available. Here we'll look at a few of the most common variations and their characteristics.

Dreadnought

The dreadnought is a large instrument with a full sound and ample bass, commonly used to accompany vocals. This is by far the most common type of acoustic guitar and is probably what most non-guitarists picture in their head when they think "acoustic guitar." Sometimes called a "Western" guitar, dreadnoughts are manufactured from many different types of wood and range in price from under a hundred to several thousand dollars (as is the case with all of the types mentioned here). The Martin D-28 is one of the most popular of all dreadnought models.

Martin D-28

Folk or Parlor Style

This guitar is much smaller in size and usually slightly quieter than a dreadnought. Due to the reduced size, the frequency response of these guitars is usually more balanced, resulting in an even, pronounced sound favored by fingerstyle players in particular. The Larrivee P-05 parlor guitar is a popular instrument in this category.

Larrivee P-05

Jumbo

As the name implies, the jumbo is the largest style of acoustic guitar and, as you might expect, produces a big, booming sound. These guitars usually have prominent bass frequencies. The sound is similar to that of a dreadnought, but often times the midrange is slightly more pronounced in a jumbo. Their timbre usually sits well within a mix of many different instruments, making them a common choice for pop artists. The Gibson SJ-200 is one such instrument commonly employed.

Gibson SJ-200

12-String

The 12-string acoustic is widely available in all of the above-mentioned styles, except for the folk style. The top two courses (pair of strings) are unisons, while the bottom four are octaves, giving this instrument a shimmering sound that can liven up the most pedestrian of strumming or fingerpicking patterns. (Leo Kottke commonly makes use of 12-strings.) Some common 12-strings include the Guild F212 XL and the Gibson J-185 12.

Guild F212 XL

OTHER OPTIONS

Aside from the size and type, there are a few other options to consider when choosing your instrument.

Cutaway

Virtually all of the above-mentioned types are available in a cutaway model. While the cutaway's effect on the sound is the subject of some debate, a well-made model shouldn't suffer any serious tonal loss. Still, the sound will be affected, however subtle the difference may be. The obvious advantage to using a cutaway model lies in its access to the higher frets. If you don't plan on reaching the topmost region of your acoustic fretboard, though, a cutaway model isn't necessary.

Alvarez cutaway

Alvarez electric acoustic

Electric Acoustic

In certain instances, practicality will be the determining factor when choosing your instrument. For instance, if you're going to be performing live with a band (like James Taylor does), you may want to look into an electric acoustic. These are available in all of the previously mentioned formats (including cutaway models) and have become arguably as popular as standard acoustics, in many circles. Electric acoustic models feature a pickup that allows you to plug into an amplifier just as you would an electric guitar. Magnetic soundhole pickups, which were among the first ones invented, are still available but not as common. The most commonly used acoustic pickup is the *piezo*, which mounts under the guitar's saddle. But increasingly, guitarists (and guitar manufacturers) are opting for complete systems—like Fishman's Aura or Taylor's Expression system—that blend pickup and microphone signals as well as acoustic imaging technology to best depict the guitar's natural acoustic tone.

Amplification

For many years, acoustic amplification lagged way behind its electric counterpart, but in recent years, several manufacturers have crafted top-notch amps made specifically for acoustic guitars. Many of these also include a channel for vocals as well, with an XLR mic input and separate level and EQ controls. These two-in-one amps are often the perfect choice for the singer-songwriter looking to play smaller venues where just a slight amount of amplification is needed. Alternatively, direct boxes are commonly employed, along with various processors (EQs, compressors, effects boxes, etc.), to plug an acoustic guitar directly into the PA. This method will also allow you to further shape the sound of the guitar, as the PA's mixer will usually possess some type of EQ as well.

Fishman Loudbox 100

If you just can't get used to the sound of a normal electric acoustic, there is another possibility for amplification: using a microphone. Generally speaking, this approach will reproduce the tone of the guitar more faithfully than any pickup can, but there are several things to consider. The first is freedom of movement. When playing with a microphone, you're going to be stuck in front of it and unable to move more than six or eight inches without losing the signal. Just a two-inch diversion will change the tone! Because of this, microphones are usually used only when sitting down. Another concern is feedback. Though a unidirectional mic, like a Shure SM57, will help with this issue, sometimes it's still necessary to enlist the help of an EQ or some type of "feedback eliminator" to identify and remove the offending frequencies. Recently, some internally (or externally) mounted microphones have become available, combining the practicality of a pickup with the sound of a mic. Though these types of systems usually run in the higher price range, using one may be your best route if you're not willing to compromise your true acoustic sound.

CONSTRUCTION AND WOOD TYPE

Probably the most significant factor contributing to the tone of an acoustic guitar is the type of wood used to build it. In addition to its sound, the wood's look and durability are also factors to consider when choosing woods. There are several commonly used woods today, and each one colors the sound in its own way. It's also quite common for a guitar to use one type of wood for the back and sides and another type for the top (soundboard).

Here is a list of some of the most commonly used woods and their characteristics:

Soundboard

Sitka spruce: Consistent, uniform grain with good overall tonal response.

Englemann spruce: A light wood in both color and weight, with a slightly louder and more "open" tone than Sitka.

Koa: Extremely beautiful grain with a predominant treble response and slightly less volume than spruce.

Western red cedar: An extremely light wood with great clarity of sound and good volume.

Genuine mahogany: A less projective wood with more emphasis on midrange.

Back and Sides

East Indian rosewood: An extremely resonant wood usually red, brown, and dark purple in color, it produces a warm bass response, especially on larger guitars.

Brazilian rosewood: Nearly extinct, therefore it's very expensive and limited in availability. The color ranges from dark brown to violet and commonly contains attractive streaks in the grain, while the tonal response is nicely balanced.

Morado: Finer in texture, but it closely resembles East Indian rosewood in appearance and tonal qualities.

Koa: A golden-brown wood with dark streaks containing slightly less bass response than rosewood and slightly less treble response than maple, but a balanced tone nonetheless.

European flamed maple: A hard, reflective wood containing an attractive rippled pattern through the grain, it produces a loud, powerful sound.

All of this information is fine and good, but it's a bit subjective. Different players have ears for different guitars, and until you get out and play one, it's hard to make a decision. If you're not able to get your hands on many guitars and demo them, try to find out what guitars are making sounds that you like on record. For instance, Bob Dylan recorded *Bringing It All Back Home* with a Gibson Nick Lucas Special. This guitar featured Brazilian rosewood for the back and sides and red Adirondak spruce for the top. The Beatles often made use of the Gibson J-160E in the early days, which featured solid Sitka spruce on the top and mahogany for the back and sides. James Taylor makes use of a custom-made Olson guitar combining a cedar top with East Indian rosewood back and sides.

Martin   Taylor   Seagull

BEFORE YOU GET STARTED

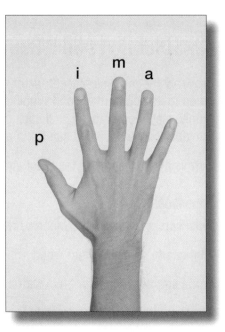

If fingerstyle is completely new to you, there are a few subjects we need to cover before diving in. If you've already spent some time with the technique, consider this section a refresher course. (Or if you're one of those people that never reads manuals, you'll most likely just skip this section.) When a guitarist begins to feel at home with the pick, he often shies away from learning to play fingerstyle because it feels like starting from scratch. This sentiment is certainly justified; it is, in a way, just like starting over again. Except this time, only *one* hand needs to learn something new.

So, first—put down that pick. You will now use only the four "picks" permanently attached to your right hand: your fingers. In fingerstyle guitar, the fingers of the right hand are identified by the following letters: *p* = thumb, *i* = index, *m* = middle, *a* = ring. These letters, derived from the Italian names for each finger, have been adopted from classical guitar notation and applied to all fingerstyle genres. What about the pinky, you ask? Because of its diminutive size, the pinky is impractical for most fingerstyle patterns. Though it's occasionally employed when plucking five-note chords (especially in jazz) and is used more extensively in the flamenco style, it doesn't see much action in the standard fingerstyle genre.

BEGINNER'S TIP

Some players prefer to use a *thumbpick* when playing fingerstyle. Whether you choose to use one or not (they can be quite handy in moving between fingerstyle and strumming quickly), all the exercises in this book still apply just the same. The thumbpick typically provides a crisper sound than the bare thumb (usually a warmer attack); it's basically a matter of personal taste, so try it both ways.

RIGHT-HAND TIPS

Just as your left hand suffered through the callous-developing process when you first learned to play, your right hand is in for a bit of discomfort. This is perfectly normal, and it will pass in time. Just be mindful of the pain—don't play until they bleed—and you should be fine.

Many fingerstyle players use the nails of their right hand, instead of the fleshy fingertips, to pluck the strings. This is another matter of taste, and each method will produce a different sound. The flesh of your fingers will produce a darker, warmer sound while nails will produce a brighter, crisper sound closer to that of a standard pick. Players who prefer nails will often grow them out a bit, thus requiring attention to care and maintenance. It's not uncommon for those players to use a nail-strengthener if they're prone to breaking. Vitamin supplements are also sometimes employed to strengthen nails. If you file your nails regularly (which most players do—especially classical guitarists), you probably won't really need to cut them anymore. The filing will keep them in good shape and at a good length. Just be sure to only file in one direction; "sawing" back and forth can actually weaken the nail.

Some experienced fingerstyle players grow their nails just long enough so that they're able to use either method, although most will usually develop a favorite and stick to it. Again, this decision is up to the individual and his or her particular taste. If you don't want to worry about taking care of your nails, then bare fingers will probably be the best option for you. Alternatively, there are some slip-on fake nails (similar to banjo fingerpicks) designed specifically for guitarists. Though some players complain about the lost physical connection with such devices, if you can get comfortable wearing them, they allow you to easily switch between the two methods.

CHAPTER 1: THE BASICS

When playing fingerstyle, your right-hand thumb (*p*) will usually handle the bottom three strings (E, A, and D), while your index (*i*), middle (*m*), and ring (*a*) fingers will handle strings 3, 2, and 1, respectively. As with any general rule, though, there are exceptions. Some players don't use their ring (*a*) finger at all, instead handling everything with *p*, *i*, and *m*. For some patterns, the *a* finger isn't necessary at all. There will be many times (even in this book) when you may need to shift your *i*, *m*, and *a* fingers to strings 4, 3, and 2, or you may use your thumb on string 3 at times. Suffice it to say, however, that your thumb will usually be handling the bass notes, and your fingers will handle the treble notes.

RIGHT-HAND POSITION

Regarding the right hand, most players will place their thumb a little more forward along the strings than the other three fingers. See the photo here for a typical right-hand position. Again, this is a general guideline; you'll find all kinds of variations from player to player. Nevertheless, it's a good starting point.

ARPEGGIOS

When you play the notes of a chord one at a time instead of all together, you're playing an *arpeggio*. This is probably the most common fingerstyle technique and therefore a good place to start. When playing the arpeggiated examples in this book, you'll want to fret the entire chord, even though the tab and notation may only show one or two notes per beat or subdivision. Fretting the whole chord is more efficient and familiar for your left hand, and it also allows the notes of the chord to ring together, which is the desired effect in most fingerpicking patterns.

Let's get started with a basic C major arpeggio pattern to get your right hand acclimated to plucking the strings. Before playing the first note in this example, you should "plant" your thumb and fingers on their respective strings so they're ready to go. Once you're in this position, begin playing the example. Try to stay relaxed and make sure that all four notes are equal in volume.

TRACK 1

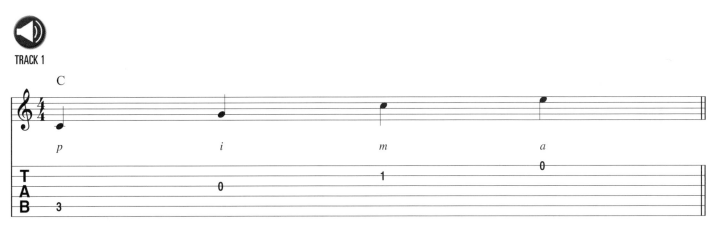

Next, let's reverse the order in which the top three strings of the arpeggio are plucked.

TRACK 1
(0:09)

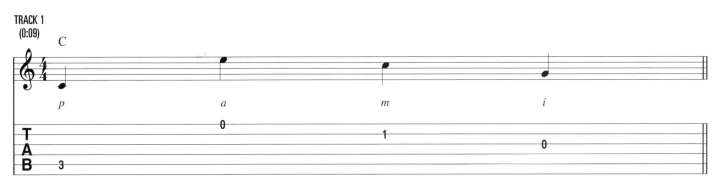

Now try these common arpeggiated variations. Each example introduces a pattern change—moving between strings with your thumb, changing direction with your fingers, and changing chords as well.

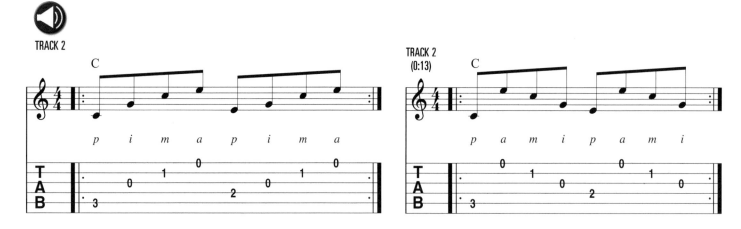

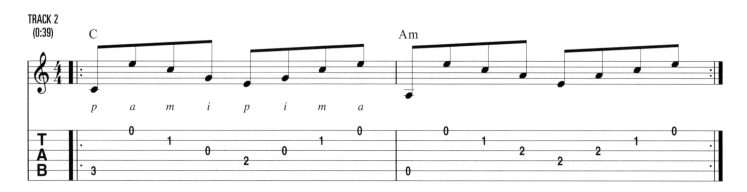

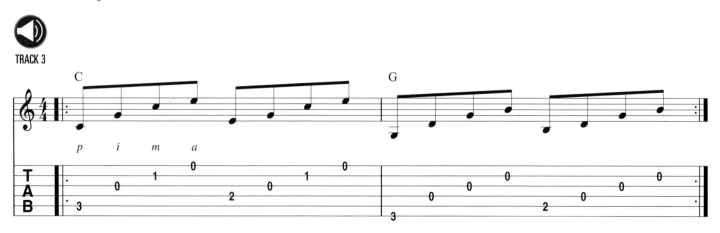

In these next examples, you'll need to shift your fingers between string groups 3-2-1 and 4-3-2. You'll also be using your thumb on string 6 for the first time.

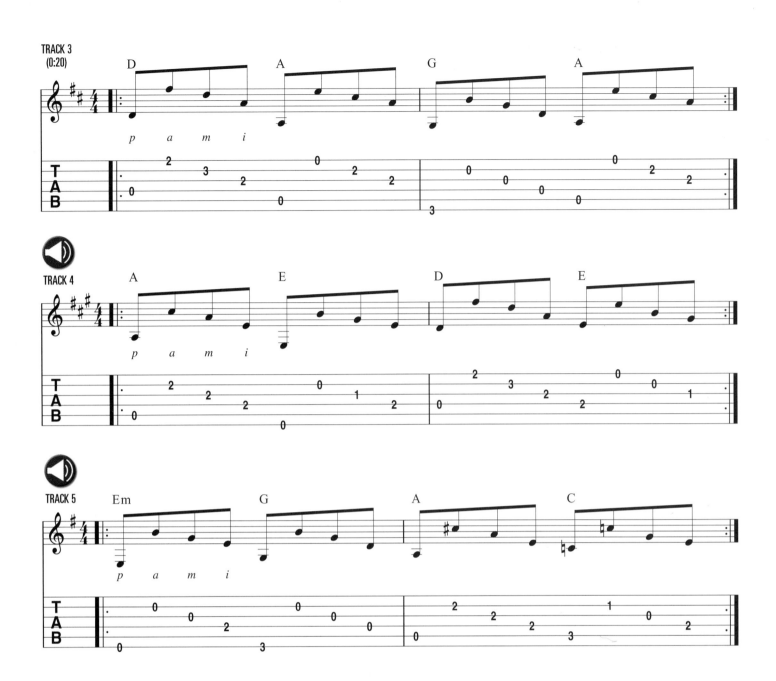

So far, so good? Great! In these four next examples, you're going to strike two notes at the same time: one bass note and one treble note. This is a very common accompaniment tool in fingerstyle guitar. Again, make sure the notes are equal in volume.

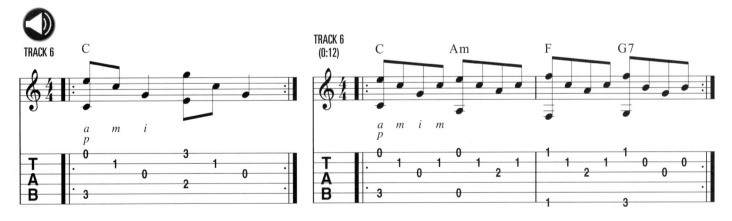

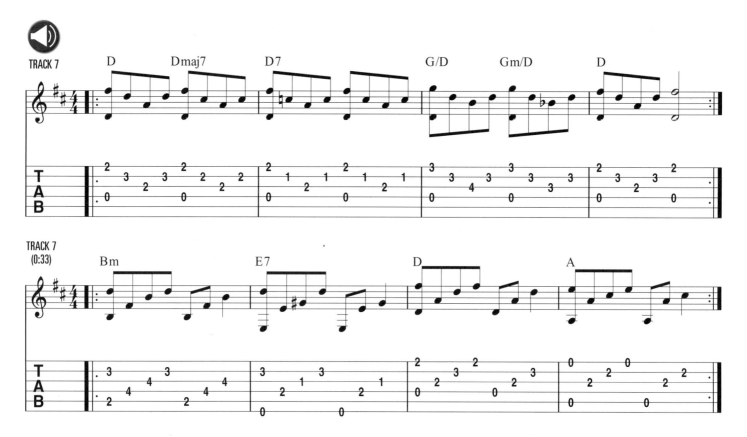

BLOCK CHORD STYLE

Though arpeggiation is an effective and pleasant-sounding accompaniment approach, there are alternative methods for navigating a chord progression using fingerstyle techniques. One of the most popular methods is called the *block chord style*, in which your right hand plucks all of the notes at once, simulating the way a pianist plays chords. Additionally, you'll sometimes want to separate the bass note from the rest of the chord, thus simulating a pianist's left- and right-hand duties. In this next example, you'll apply the block chord style to a C major chord, first with a separate bass (C) note, and then as one whole chord.

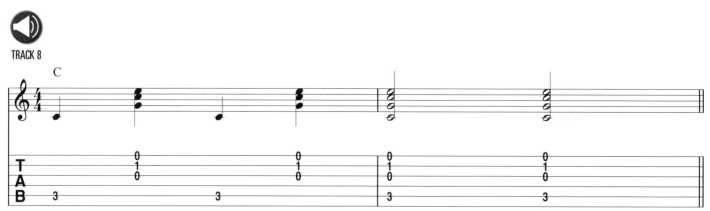

Listen closely to make sure that all of the notes are ringing out clearly. It's not uncommon for some fingers to just "go along for the ride" in the beginning, resulting in a buried or nonexistent note. If you find that you're experiencing this problem, try breaking up the chord into different two-note combinations until the balance in volume is better. Here's an exercise that will help:

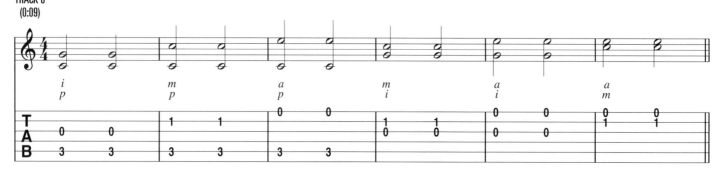

Once you're able to achieve balance between all the notes, try the following examples. In the last two examples, the thumb fills in some space with a few bass notes in between the chords. This is a common variation on the block chord style.

TRACK 9

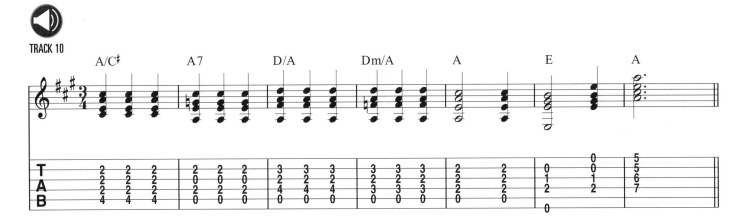

TRACK 10

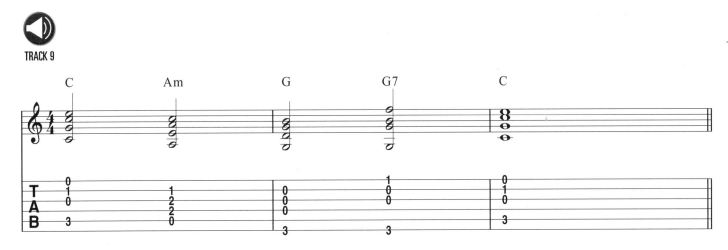

TRACK 11

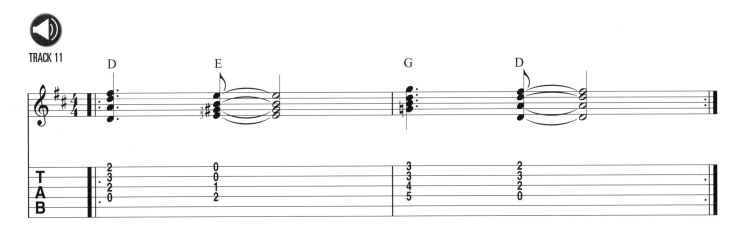

TRACK 12

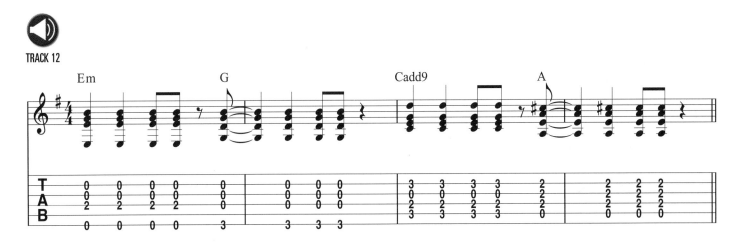

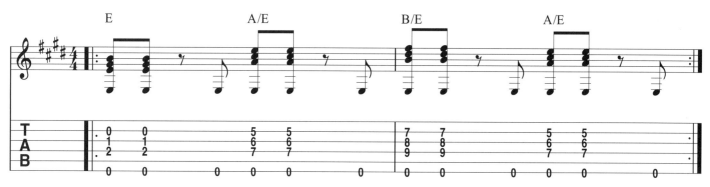

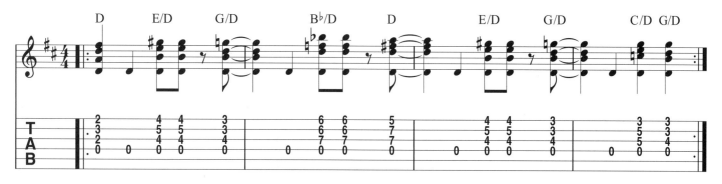

CHAPTER 2: ACCOMPANIMENT STYLES

Now that your fingers have tested the fingerstyle waters, let's dive right into some accompaniment styles, focusing on the techniques commonly used to accompany vocals. In this chapter, we'll further explore arpeggiation and block chord styles, but first we're going to dip into the most popular fingerstyle accompaniment technique of all: Travis picking.

TRAVIS PICKING

Arguably the most commonly employed technique in the entire fingerstyle world is *Travis picking*. Named for country guitar legend Merle Travis and made requisite by the great Chet Atkins, Travis picking usually involves the thumb alternating between two bass notes while the remaining fingers "fill in the holes" on the melody side.

This first example demonstrates a basic Travis picking pattern that should help you get a feel for the technique. Be sure to follow the picking directions between the notation and tab staves, as your thumb is responsible for plucking the notes on strings 5 and 4.

TRACK 15

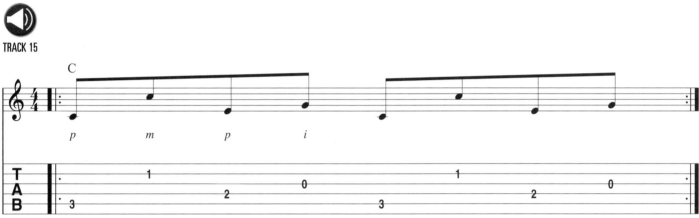

Notice that the thumb always plucks its notes on the downbeat, rocking back and forth between two strings. This steady pulse serves as the backbone to many variations on the Travis picking style. Regardless of what your fingers are doing, the thumb will almost always keep chugging away on the beat with alternating bass notes.

In the next example, we're moving between C and G chords, which brings a new challenge. When you reach the G chord, your thumb rocks back and forth between strings 6 and 4. If you have trouble skipping string 5 cleanly, isolate the bass line and practice just that move until it becomes second nature. It should also be noted that, in Travis picking patterns such as these, the "and" of beat 2 is often slightly accented to provide gentle syncopation that helps to create a sense of momentum.

TRACK 15
(0:09)

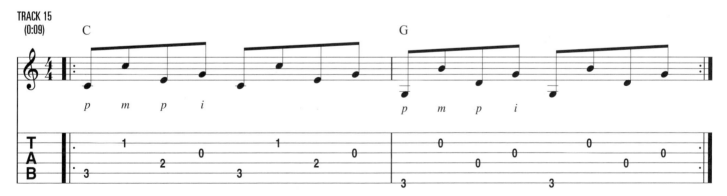

There are literally countless variations on the basic Travis picking pattern, but we'll look at a few of the more useful ones here. In example A, we're simply plucking the first two notes on beat 1 at the same time, creating a quarter note instead of two eighth notes. In example B, the right-hand thumb is working overtime, substituting the low 5th for the root on beat 3. Example C omits the first treble note altogether, beginning only with a quarter-note bass root on beat 1. Example D elaborates on C, making use of the *a* finger to create an interesting pattern. Finally, examples E and F introduce a right-hand shift to a higher string group, which is another option when accessing higher strings. Notice also the tie in example F, which further accents the "and" of beat 2.

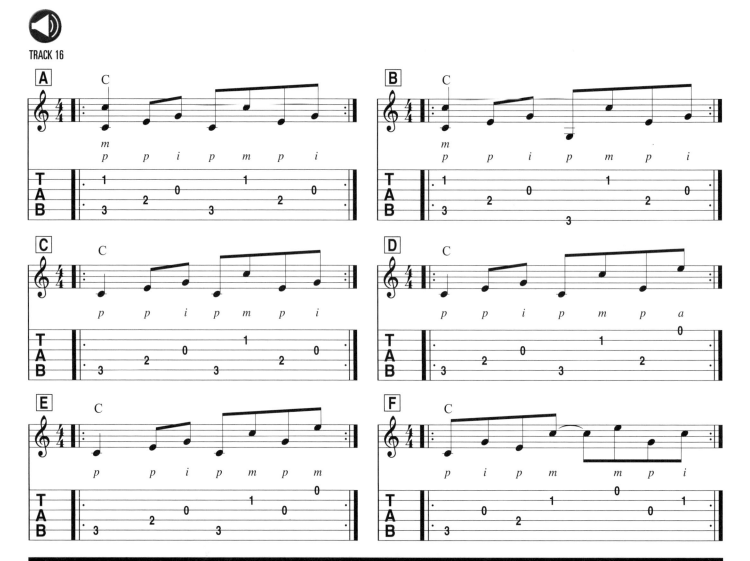

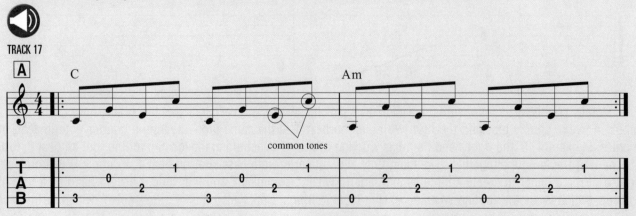

Transitioning Smoothly Between Chords

When playing fingerstyle, especially when Travis picking or arpeggiating, you'll need to focus a bit more on the transition between chords than you do when strumming with a pick. If you're not careful, some patterns can sound unmusical due to abrupt gaps in sound when refretting for a new chord. This is much more apparent in fingerstyle because you're usually dealing with notes that are struck individually and are therefore more conspicuous when clipped short. There are a few strategies that can help you avoid this pitfall.

Common Tones

Often times, two chords will share one or more notes. These are called *common tones*. If you're able to fret a common tone with the same finger for two consecutive chords, you'll experience a smoother transition between the chords. In familiar chord shapes like C and Am (example A), it occurs quite naturally. But on occasion, you may find it advantageous to alter a chord fingering to maintain the common tone. In example B, for example, notice the alternate fingering for the D chord, which facilitates the common F♯ and D tones.

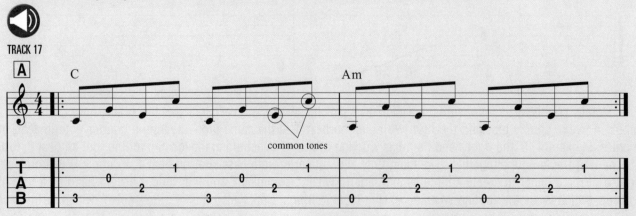

14

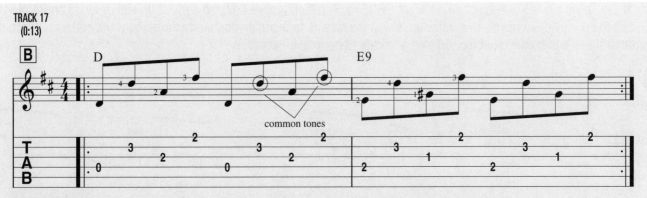

Partial Fretting

Since you're often only striking one or two notes at a time when fingerpicking, you don't always need to fret the entire chord on the downbeat as you do when strumming. Often times you'll only need to fret the bass note on beat 1, leaving you extra time to fret the rest of the chord. This can cut down on unmusical gaps when there are no common tones, allowing you to sustain the treble note right up to the point when the new bass note is struck. In example A below, you have until the "and" of beat 1 before you have to fret anything for the E chord. This means you can sustain the C# from the previous A chord right up to the moment when you strike the low E string. In example B, barring all six strings with your first finger presents the same half-beat window of time with which to fret the G#m chord.

TRACK 18

Omission

If there is simply no way to bridge two chords smoothly—such as when position shifts are required—your best option may be to omit the final treble note of the measure and instead end the measure with a bass quarter note played by the thumb. Omitting the final eighth note in these instances makes the gap much less noticeable. For instance, in example A below, you're required to shift to fret 4 instantly for the C#m, since the final note of measure 1 is an A on fret 2. Though it's not impossible, it is very difficult to pull off smoothly. In example B, however, we omit that final eighth note (A), and the effect is a bit less jarring.

TRACK 19

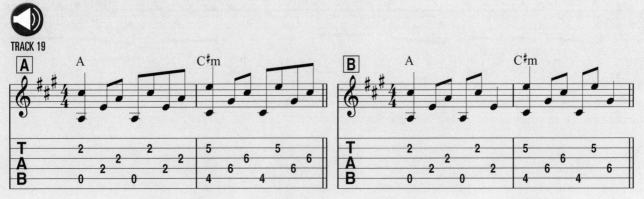

Now try these Travis picking examples, which combine all the variations we've covered so far, but with different chord progressions. Keep the transition concepts in mind when switching chords to maintain continuity throughout the patterns. Try to spot the common tones and then exploit them, using alternate fingerings if necessary.

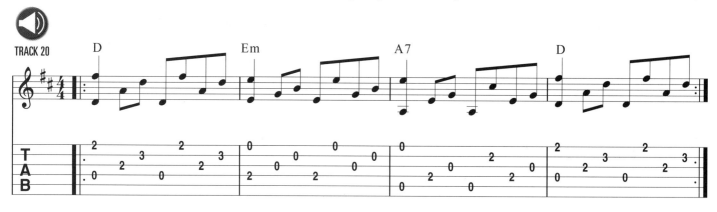

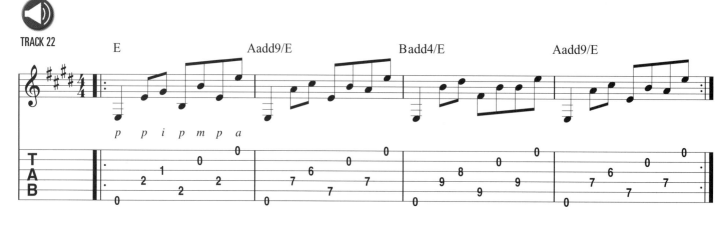

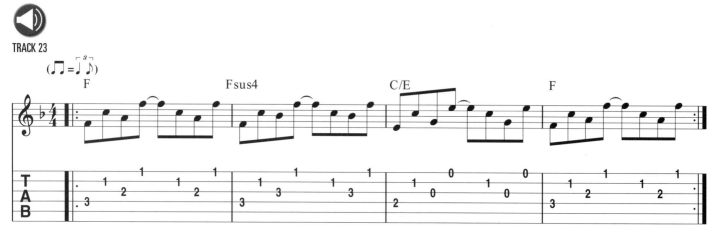

*T = Thumb on 6th string

**Strum w/ thumb.

Here are a few classic Travis picking examples from the pros.

DUST IN THE WIND

TRACK 26

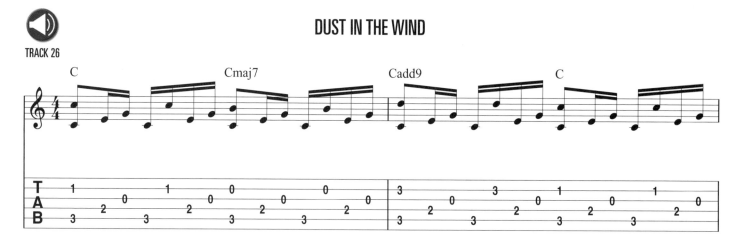

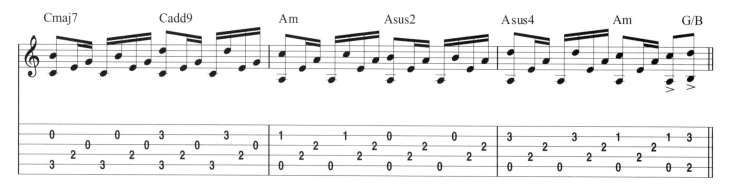

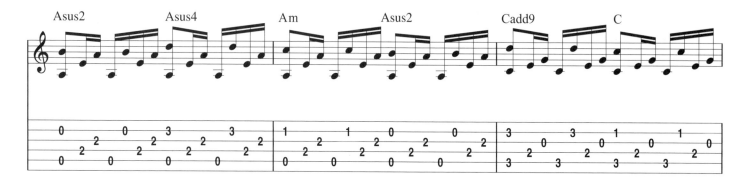

TAKE ME HOME, COUNTRY ROADS

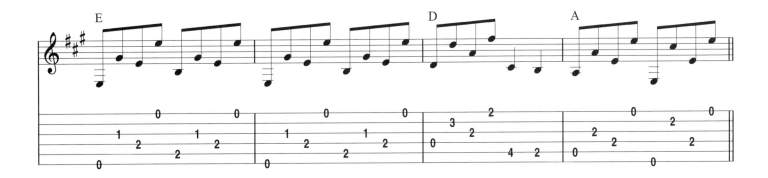

YOU WERE MEANT FOR ME

TRACK 27

Lyrics by JEWEL KILCHER
Music by JEWEL KILCHER and STEVE POLTZ
© 1995, 1996 EMI APRIL MUSIC INC., WIGGLY TOOTH MUSIC, THIRD STORY MUSIC, INC., ROBERT DUFFY MUSIC and POLIO BOY MUSIC
All Rights for WIGGLY TOOTH MUSIC Controlled and Administered by EMI APRIL MUSIC INC.
All Rights Reserved   International Copyright Secured   Used by Permission

GHOST

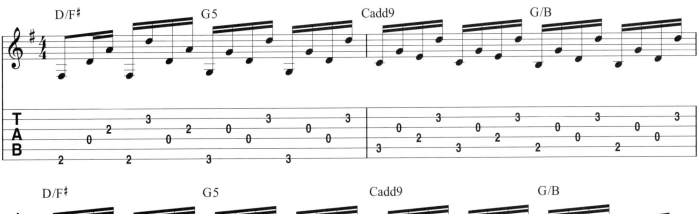

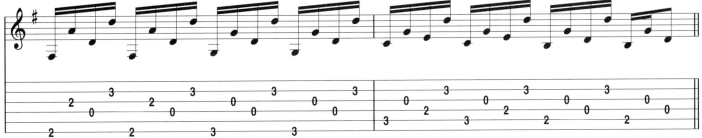

Words and Music by EMILY SALIERS
© 1992 EMI VIRGIN SONGS, INC. and GODHAP MUSIC
All Rights Controlled and Administered by EMI VIRGIN SONGS, INC.
All Rights Reserved   International Copyright Secured   Used by Permission

ARPEGGIATION

Another common fingerstyle approach, especially on ballads, is to *arpeggiate* the chords in a rolling fashion. We touched on this technique a little bit in Chapter 1. Now we'll examine it a bit more thoroughly.

Our first example comprises C and G chords arpeggiated simply in ascending fashion. Remember to sustain the C note on the "and" of beat 4 in measure 1 right up until you strike the low G note on the downbeat of measure 2, to avoid an unwanted gap between the chords.

It's also common to combine arpeggiation with simultaneously struck chord clusters.

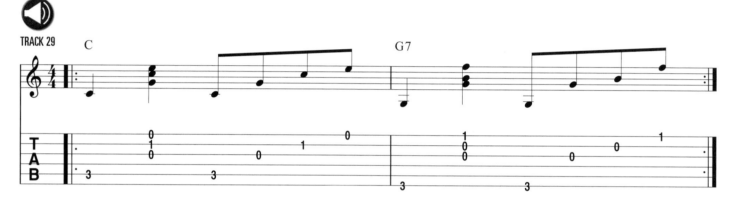

By alternating bass notes, descending through the arpeggios as well as ascending, and adding simultaneously struck notes, we can create further and more interesting fingerstyle patterns, as shown in the following examples.

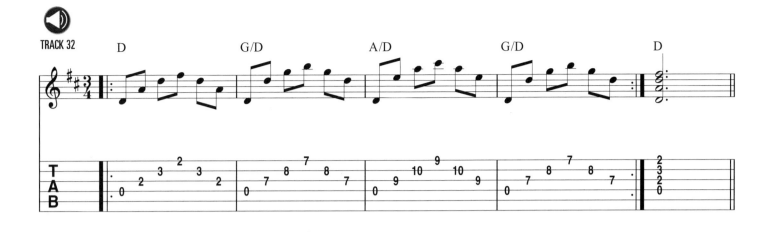

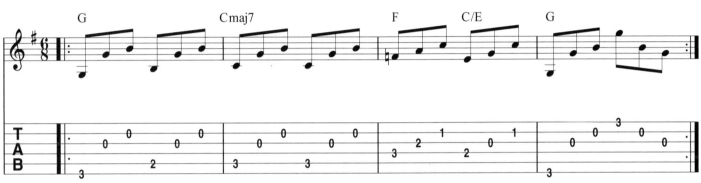

TRACK 35

*Strum w/ thumb.

Ornamental Devices

As you delve ever deeper into fingerstyle guitar, you'll find the need or desire to spice up your arpeggiation or Travis picking patterns, as it's those subtleties that often make the difference between a merely functional fingerpicking riff and one that really shines. Fortunately, there are some easy methods you can use to achieve that brilliant sound.

Hammer-ons and Pull-offs

One easy way to add zest to a fingerstyle pattern is to use hammer-ons and pull-offs. In example A, we use hammer-ons from B to C and pull-offs from D to C to liven up a basic Travis picking riff. Example B applies the same concept to G and Cmaj7 arpeggios.

TRACK 36

*T = Thumb on 6th string

Melodic Connections

Alternatively, you can temporarily break up a fingerpicking pattern with a well-placed melody or passing tone to add another piece of "ear candy" for the listener. This is common in James Taylor's playing. Example A interjects melodies on beats 3 and 4—first on the treble side, and then the bass. In example B, we're connecting the chords with an ascending quarter-note melody harmonized in 10ths (beats 3–4 of measures 1 and 3).

TRACK 37

Let's take a look at a few songs that make use of arpeggiation. Notice the use of the ornamental devices we looked at.

WHEN THE CHILDREN CRY

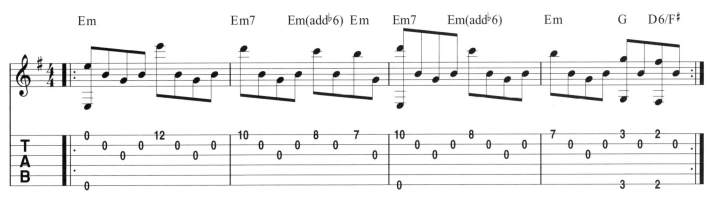

ANNIE'S SONG

STRONG ENOUGH

TRACK 38

FRIENDS IN LOW PLACES

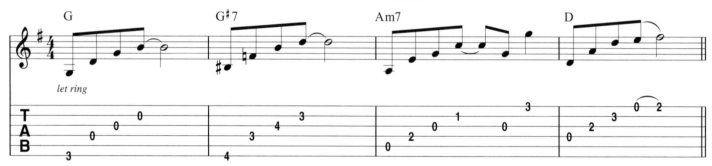

YOU'VE GOT A FRIEND

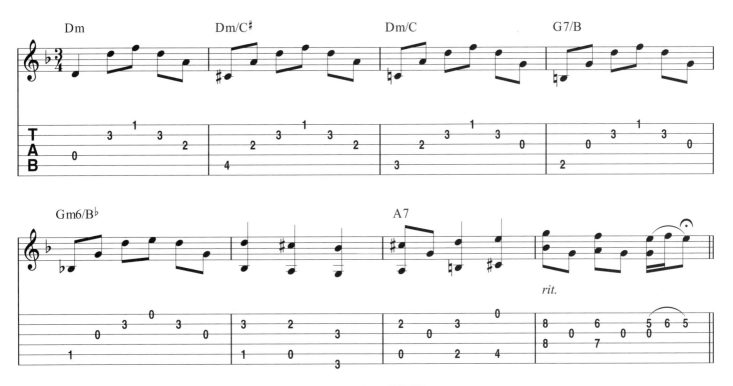

BLOCK CHORD STYLE

Aside from Travis picking and arpeggiation, you'll occasionally see the block chord style, which we also spent a little time with in Chapter 1. Let's take a look at how we can expand on this approach.

To review, here's a basic example of the block chord style. The right-hand thumb handles the bass notes, and the fingers (*i*, *m*, and *a*) pluck all the treble notes.

TRACK 39

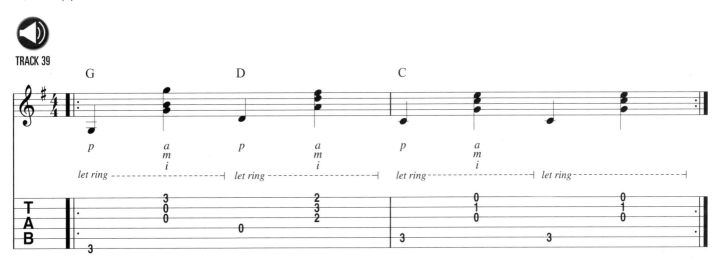

Sounds pretty simple, right? But add a little syncopation and some make-do percussive sounds, and we can turn the previous example into a grooving little riff. The "X" notes on beats 2 and 4 are accomplished by simply "planting" your right-hand fingers on the appropriate strings with much more force than normal. On beat 2 of measure 1, for example, you would bring your right hand down in preparation for the following D chord, with your thumb ready to strike the fourth string and your fingers on the three treble strings. But you would do this with a quick, forceful motion so that the strings slap against the frets and sound the desired percussive "smack."

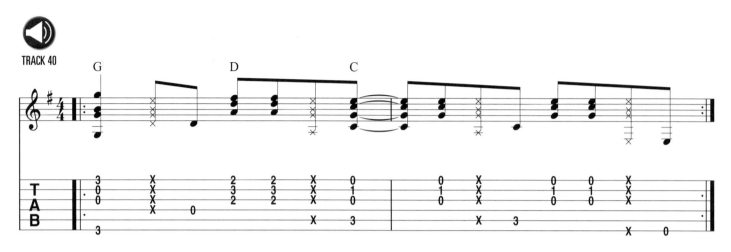

In essence, the percussive sound on beats 2 and 4 is simulating a snare-drum backbeat. This simple ornament can really add another dimension to an accompanying guitar part. Try the following examples to help get the technique under your fingers.

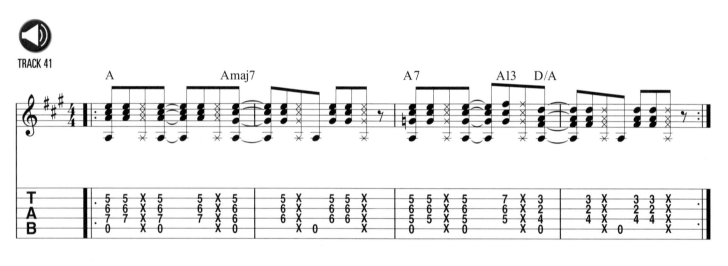

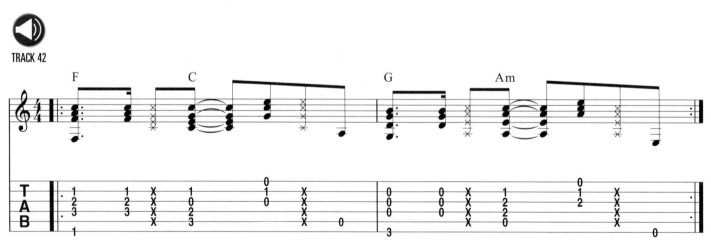

Here we see two classic block chord style riffs.

YESTERDAY

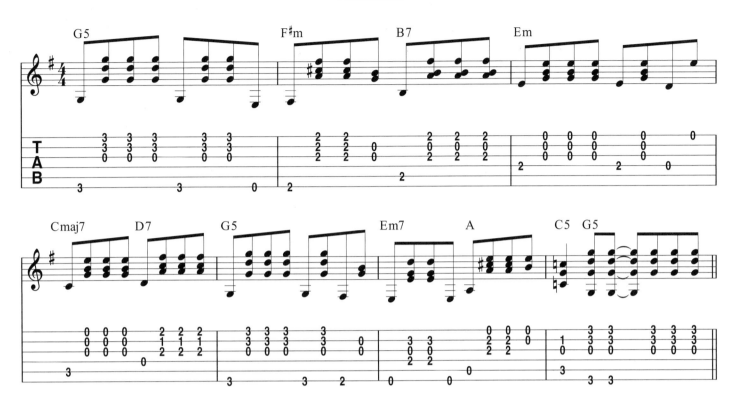

MORE THAN WORDS

TRACK 43

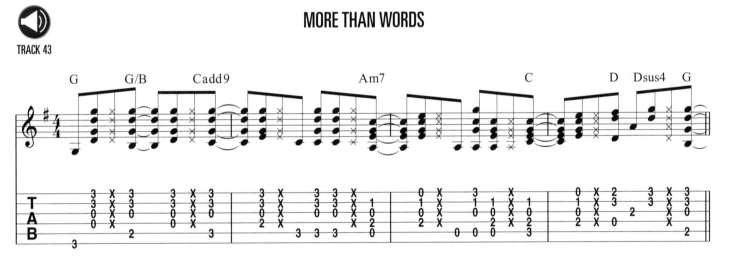

CHAPTER 3: RIGHT HAND INDEPENDENCE

One benefit of the fingerstyle method is its capability for sounding like two or more instruments playing at the same time. This is particularly handy when performing solo guitar arrangements, in which you can play a melody on the top strings with your fingers while playing a bass line on the low strings with your thumb. This isn't easy to do, however, and you'll need to develop *right hand independence* to fully capitalize on this benefit.

Right hand independence simply means the ability to play different rhythms with the different fingers of your right hand. The most critical independence lies between your thumb and the rest of your fingers. It's absolutely essential that you're able to separate them, rhythmically speaking. There will also be times when your *i*, *m*, and *a* fingers will need independence from each other as well, but by far the most common task at hand will involve the thumb being separated from one or more of the other fingers.

Let's take a look at a basic example to demonstrate the concept.

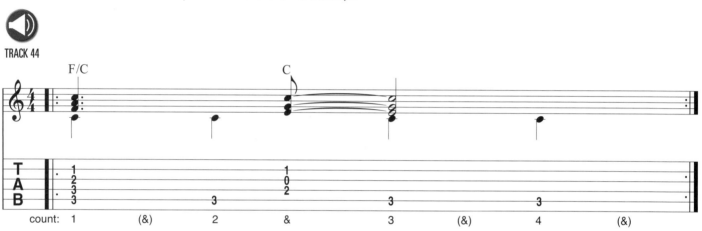

Most beginning fingerstyle players will want to restrike the bass note along with the chord on the "and" of beat 2. This is what the concept of right hand independence is all about. You need to be able to separate the roles of the bass and treble so that they're free to do whatever is required of them. Try the above example again, and really concentrate on making the bass note fall solidly on the downbeat. It's the time-keeper in this instance.

When you've gotten the hang of the previous example, try these next ones. You'll encounter several different rhythms, so work them out slowly at first. Your thumb will be keeping steady quarter notes throughout each example, playing the downstemmed notes, while your fingers handle all the upstemmed notes. (Note: *Some of the exercises in this book have been notated with downstemmed bass notes to help underscore the concept of right hand independence. In practical application, however, all of the notes are sometimes stemmed the same way, as it's somewhat implied that the notes will ring together throughout the duration of the measure.*)

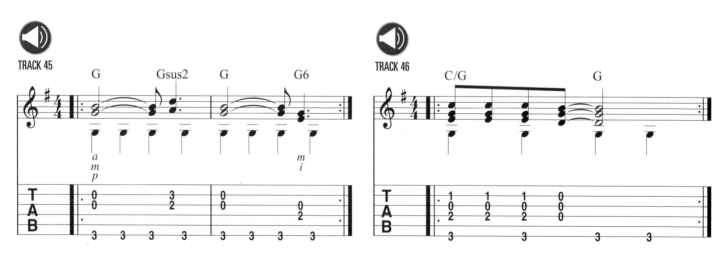

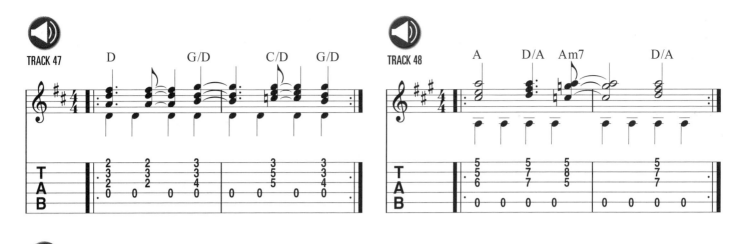

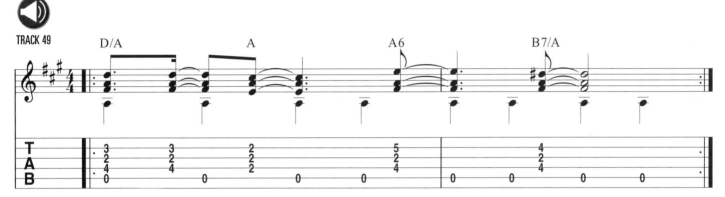

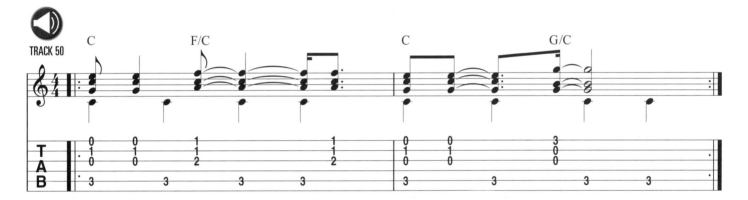

Now let's add some arpeggiation to the treble parts. The thumb still keeps a steady quarter-note pulse, but the bass notes will change in a few examples. Take your time especially on the last two examples. The three-against-four feel is an especially tricky rhythm for your picking fingers.

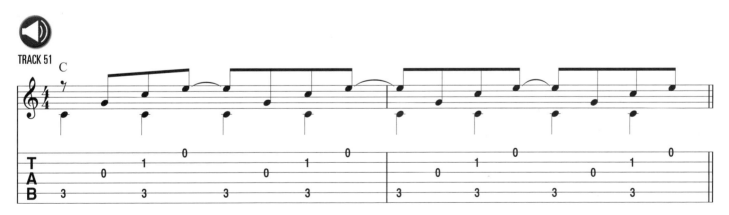

TRACK 51
(0:11)

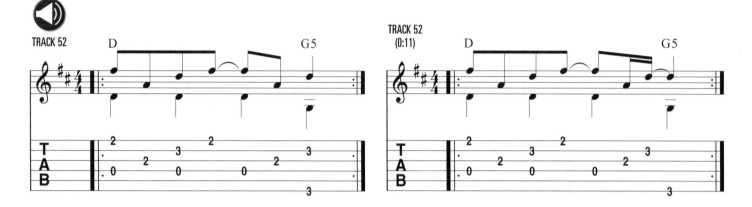

TRACK 52

TRACK 52
(0:11)

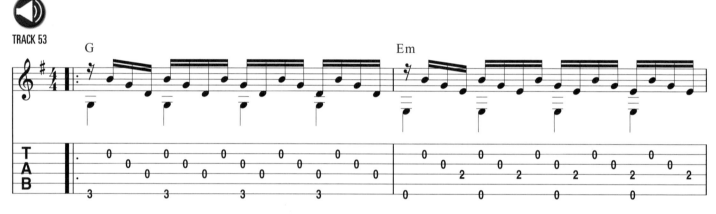

TRACK 53

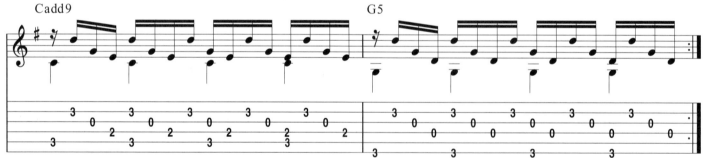

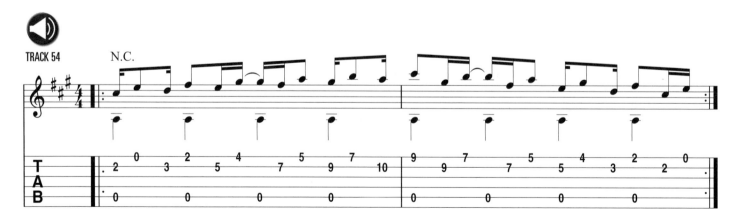

TRACK 54

For even more challenging—and interesting—parts, toss some hammer-ons and pull-offs into the phrases, as in these next few examples. Remember to start out slowly! Don't speed up until your hammered and pulled notes sound as loudly as the picked ones.

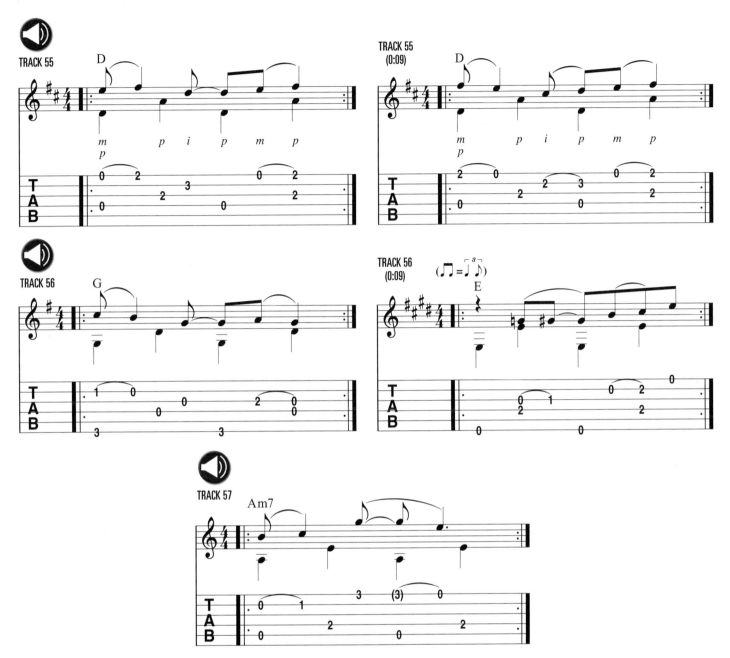

These final examples will feature a melody on the top and a steady bass on the bottom. Again, think of your thumb as the time-keeper; it pounds out steady quarter notes no matter what's going on up top.

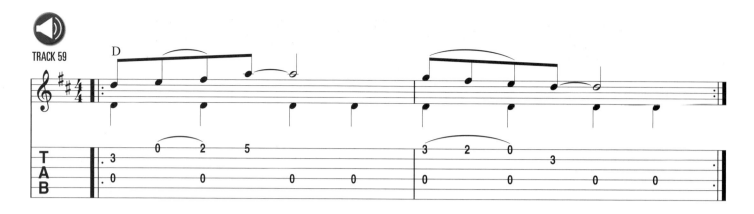

TRACK 59

TRACK 60

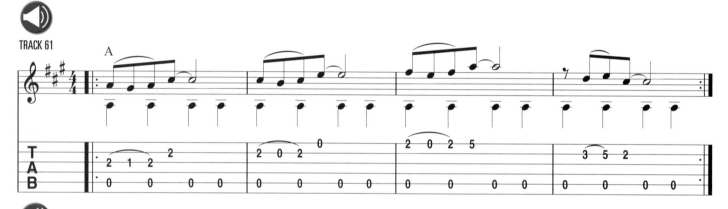

TRACK 61

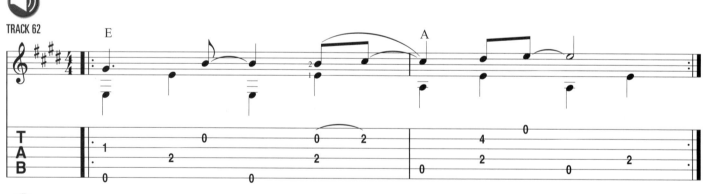

TRACK 62

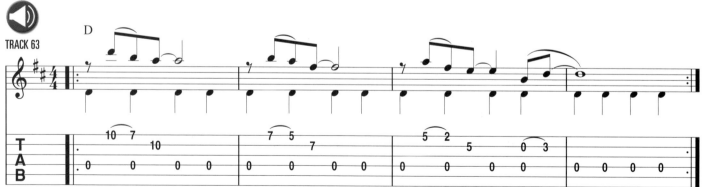

TRACK 63

CHAPTER 4: ARRANGING FOR SOLO GUITAR—PART 1

One of the most enjoyable aspects of fingerstyle guitar is being able to play solo arrangements of songs. (This is a prime example of where that right hand independence comes in.) Solo guitar arrangements can range from simple to incredibly complex, so we'll start at ground zero in this chapter and work our way up. We'll take a look at some more ambitious arrangements in Chapter 7.

THE MELODY

When building any arrangement, it's best to start with the melody. This way, you'll know up front if there's anything for which you'll need to make special accommodations—an usually large range, harmonized melody notes, key changes, and so forth.

Choosing a Key

The first thing you'll need to do when arranging any song is choose a key that sits well on the guitar. It's extremely common to change the original key of a song when arranging for guitar, due to the various idiosyncrasies and limitations of the instrument. Open-string keys (C, G, D, A, E) usually work best, but if you need the arrangement to be in a specific non-friendly guitar key for whatever reason, there are ways to handle that as well. (Capos are particularly helpful in those instances, and we'll take a look at them in the next chapter.)

Let's start by creating a solo arrangement of the evergreen Christmas hymn "Silent Night," in the guitar-friendly key of G. We'll be able to play most of the melody (which has a range of an octave and a 4th) in open position, but we'll need to shift just a few times due to the large interval span. Generally speaking, it's best to take advantage of open strings whenever possible with solo arrangements, as it provides an opportunity to shift, if need be, or change bass notes (or chords in more complex arrangements). Here's a look at the original melody and how it could most easily be played.

SILENT NIGHT

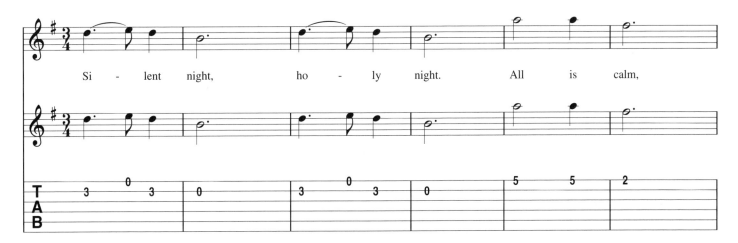

Words by JOSEPH MOHR
Translated by JOHN F. YOUNG
Music by FRANZ X. GRUBER
Copyright © 2008 by HAL LEONARD CORPORATION
International Copyright Secured   All Rights Reserved

all is bright. Round yon vir - gin, moth - er and child.

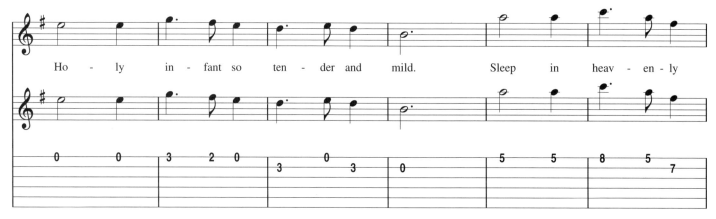

Ho - ly in - fant so ten - der and mild. Sleep in heav - en - ly

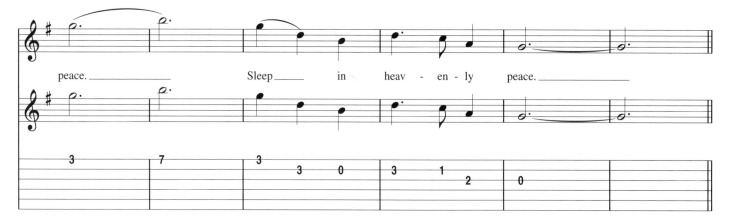

peace._____ Sleep_____ in heav - en - ly peace._____

THE BASS

The next logical step is to add the bass notes. We won't start with anything fancy—just whole notes for the most part (or in this case of 3/4 time, dotted half notes). Notice the shift to fifth position in measure 17.

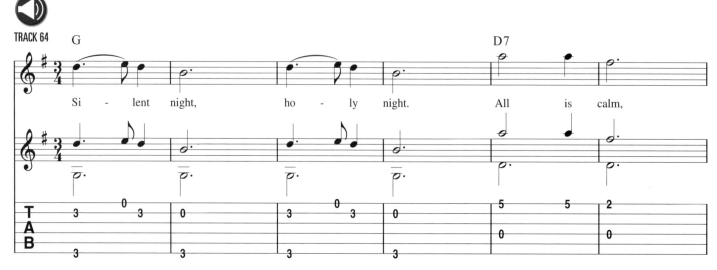

TRACK 64   G   D7

Si - lent night, ho - ly night. All is calm,

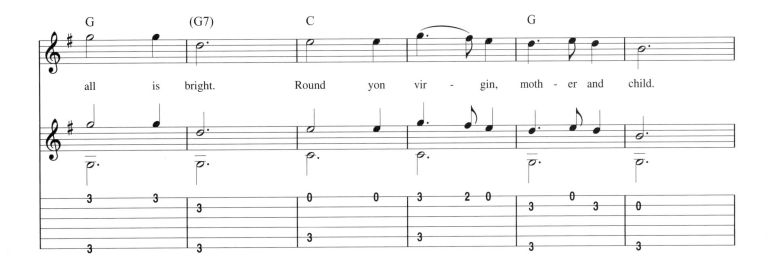

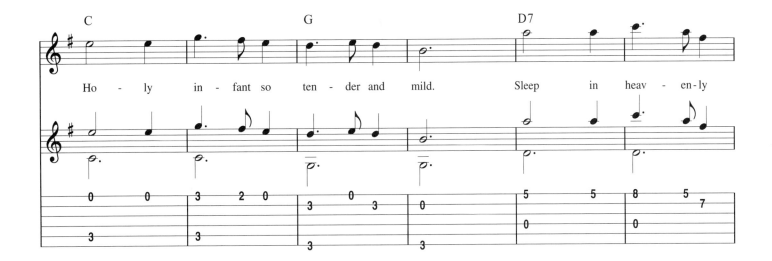

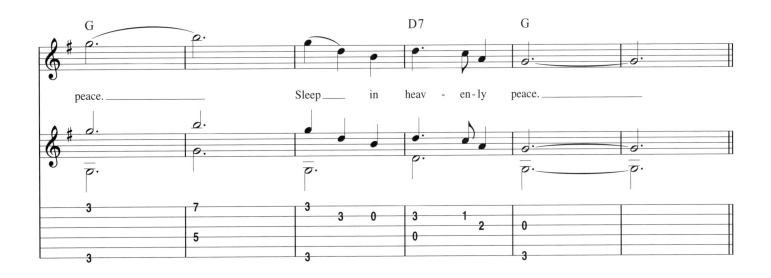

Once you've got the hang of that, you can fill out the arrangement by playing quarter notes with the bass. This is great practice for that right hand independence you studied in Chapter 3. Notice we've made use of a few "walking" bass lines to add pizzazz to a few chord changes.

TRACK 65

G D7
Si - lent night, ho - ly night. All is calm,
G G7 C G G7
all is bright. Round yon vir - gin, moth - er and child.
C G D7
Ho - ly in - fant so ten - der and mild. Sleep in heav - en-ly
G D7 G
peace. Sleep in heav - en-ly peace.
TAB

THE FINISHING TOUCHES

At this point, there are a few more choices available for fleshing out a simple arrangement. Depending upon the song's structure, tempo, and meter, it's up to you to decide which one will work best. Often, it's best to experiment with different methods until you're satisfied with the result. Let's take a look at a few of these approaches.

Filling in the Gaps

Perhaps the easiest method is to simply add some filler in between melody notes. This is just an expansion on the bass/melody style. The basic idea is to fill in the space left when the melody comes to rest. This is usually accomplished using arpeggiated notes from the chord, but other options, such as a walking bass line, may also be used. Generally speaking, your thumb will still play only the bass notes, and your fingers will handle the melody and filler notes, though there are times when the thumb works for the filler notes as well. We'll see plenty of examples that use this method later in this chapter, but here's a sample of what "Silent Night" may sound like with this approach. Notice the walking bass line in the last measure that leads right into C.

TRACK 66

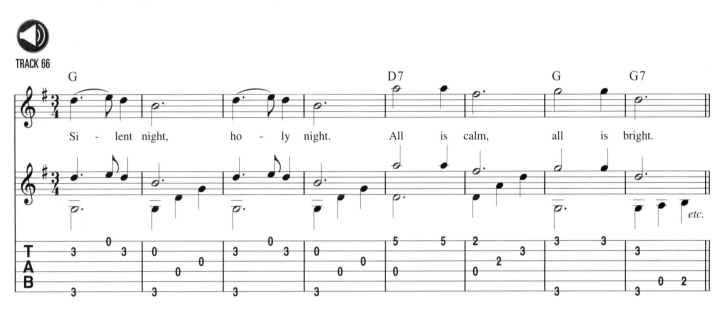

Block Chord Style

Another option in building solo arrangements is to play chords, always placing the melody note on top. This method is very commonly used in jazz solo arrangements. The arrangement can range from one chord per measure to a different chord for each melody note. You'll often need to re-situate the melody in different positions to allow certain chord voicings to be played beneath it. This is what "Silent Night" might sound like with this method.

TRACK 66
(0:22)

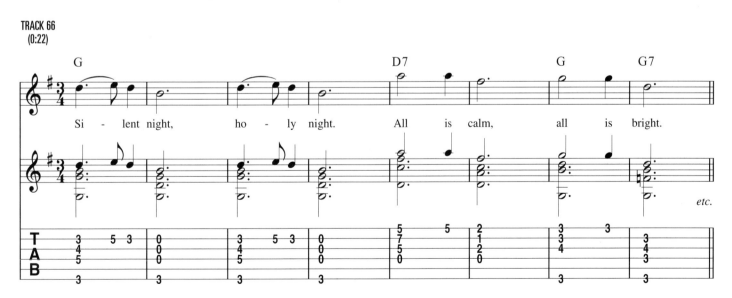

Alternating Bass Notes

If the song's melody is somewhat active, simple arrangements, with just an alternating bass note played by the thumb similar to that found in Travis picking patterns, work just fine. This method generally sounds best on 4/4 songs, although there are variations that can be used with 3/4 as well. One variation might be to simply arpeggiate the bass notes of a chord with the thumb, in a quarter-note rhythm. Just as with the block chord style, you may have to experiment with placing the melody in different spots to facilitate the bass line. Here's a sample of what "Silent Night" might sound like using that approach.

TRACK 66
(0:42)

Melodic and Harmonic Adjustments

Melodic Rhythm

There are times, especially in easy arrangements, when you may need to simplify the rhythm of a melody to make the arrangement more playable, or to suit a certain feel or meter you've selected for the arrangement. This is very common, and you'll see this in several arrangements later in this chapter. For instance, in "Silent Night," you may want to change the rhythm of this line:

This type of rhythmic adjustment to the melody is left to the discretion of the arranger. And though it's nice to think that you will become technically proficient enough to handle any kind of rhythm the melody can throw at you, there may still be times when it's just too difficult to get it exactly right without making some sort of compromise in the arrangement. You'll need to decide what the most important element is in those instances and make the adjustment that best serves the arrangement.

Reharmonization

Reharmonization is a great tool for making a melody sound fresh and new again. It's beyond the scope of this book to cover this concept in detail, but we can cover some basics. When you reharmonize a melody, you simply place a different chord beneath it, rather than the standard harmony. The sky is really the limit when it comes to choosing a new harmony, but generally speaking you don't want it to clash with the melody note. For example, if you were in the key of G, G minor wouldn't be a logical choice to reharmonize a B note, since the G minor chord contains a B♭. However, Em (B = 5th), Bm (B = root), Cmaj7 (B = 7th), or even A9 (B = 9th) might all work well.

Using "Silent Night" as our example again, you might choose to reharmonize this phrase:

TRACK 67

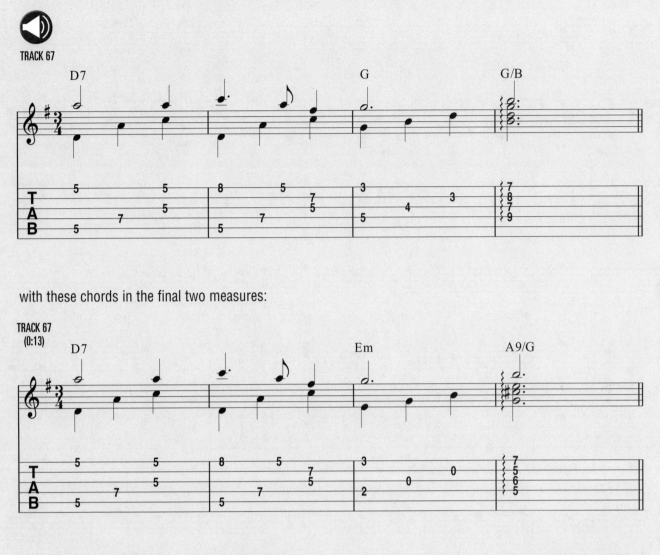

with these chords in the final two measures:

TRACK 67
(0:13)

Your personal taste as well as your knowledge of harmony will be the deciding factors when reharmonizing. Don't be afraid to experiment with this powerful technique; it can invigorate even the most mundane arrangements and help to provide your own personal touch.

All of these methods and techniques (filling in the gaps, block chord style, reharmonization) are often combined in the same arrangement. This is a great way, for instance, to set two verses apart from each other. So with that knowledge in hand, let's put it all together to create one last complete arrangement of "Silent Night."

Si - lent night, ho - ly night. All is calm,

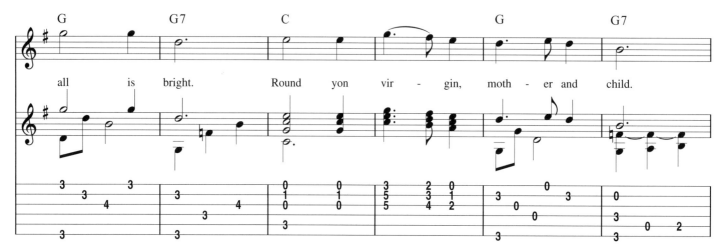

all is bright. Round yon vir - gin, moth - er and child.

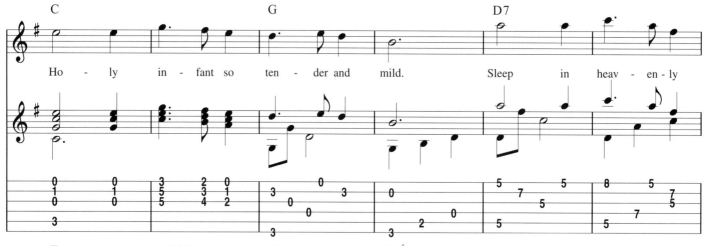

Ho - ly in - fant so ten - der and mild. Sleep in heav - en - ly

peace._____ Sleep___ in heav - en - ly peace._____

Now let's take a look at some arrangements of popular songs. Try to spot the different arrangement techniques at work.

YESTERDAY

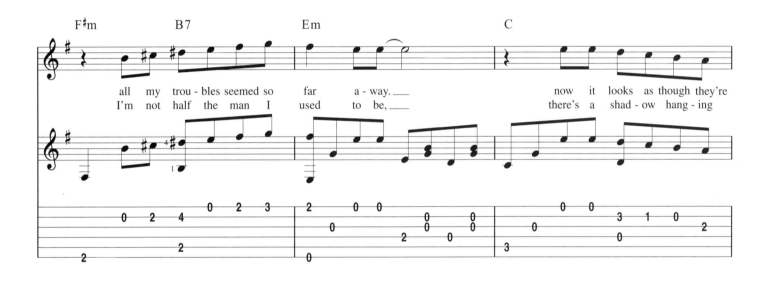

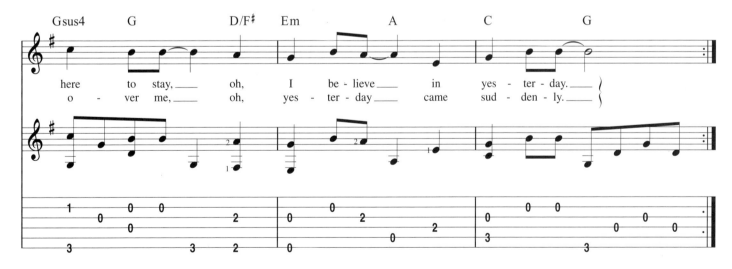

Bridge

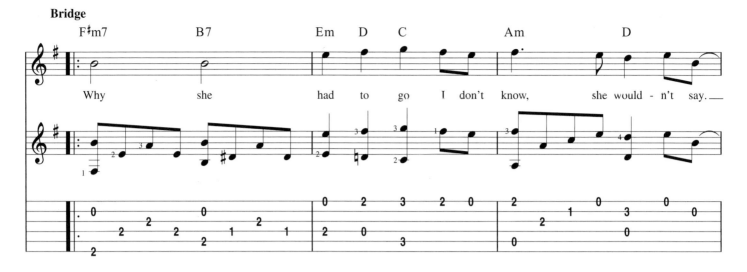

Why she had to go I don't know, she would - n't say. —

— I said some - thing wrong, now I

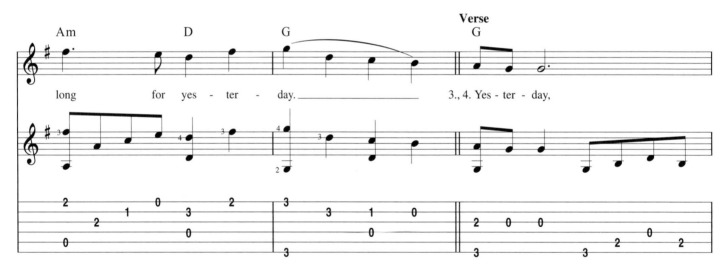

long for yes - ter - day. _____ 3., 4. Yes - ter - day,

Verse

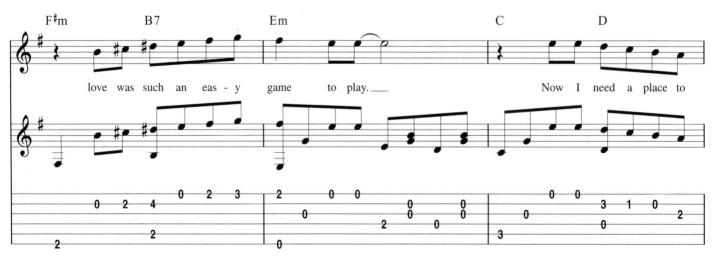

love was such an eas - y game to play. — Now I need a place to

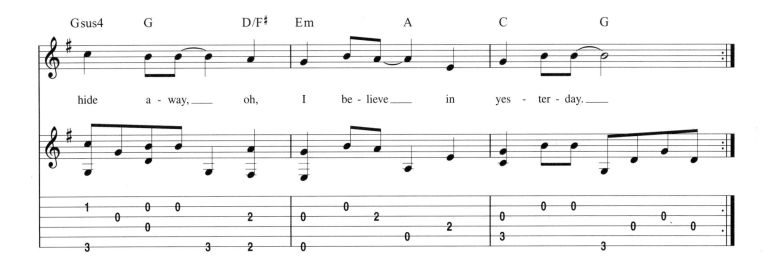

hide a - way, _____ oh, I be - lieve _____ in yes - ter - day. _____

Outro

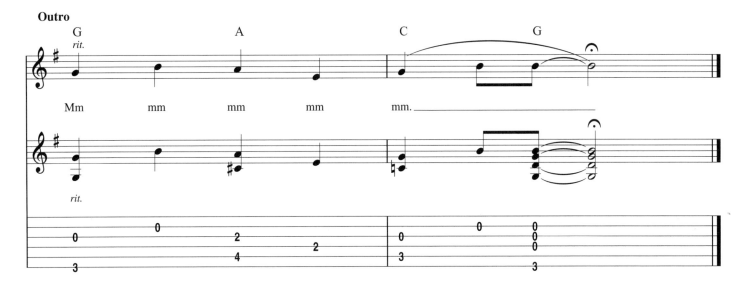

Mm mm mm mm mm. _____

TRACK 70

GEORGIA ON MY MIND

Verse

Slowly ♩ = 70

1., 2. Geor - gia, _____ Geor - gia, _____ the whole day through. Just an old sweet song keeps

Outro

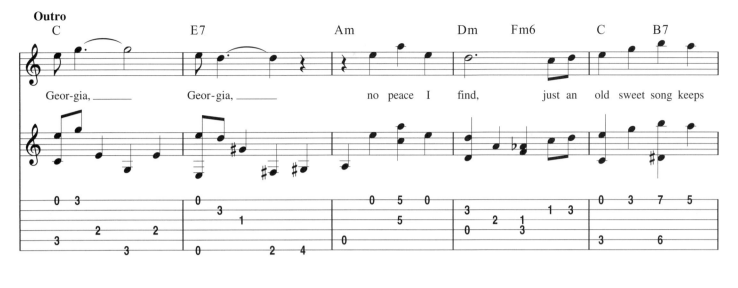

Geor-gia,_____ Geor-gia,_____ no peace I find, just an old sweet song keeps

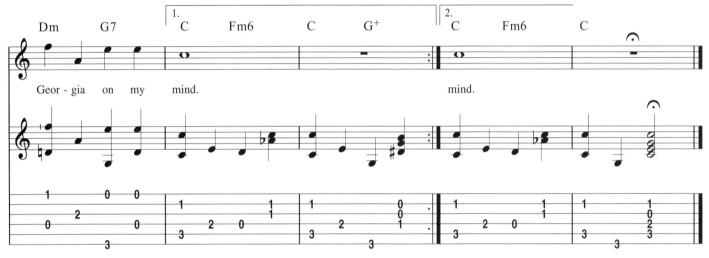

Geor - gia on my mind. mind.

TRACK 71

MY FAVORITE THINGS
from The Sound of Music

Verse

Lively, with spirit ♩ = 126

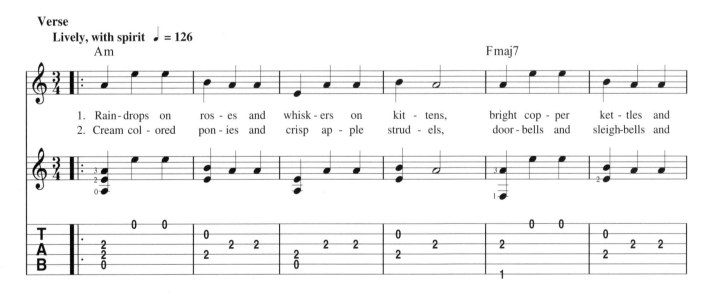

1. Rain-drops on ros - es and whisk - ers on kit - tens, bright cop - per ket - tles and
2. Cream col - ored pon - ies and crisp ap - ple strud - els, door - bells and sleigh-bells and

Lyrics by OSCAR HAMMERSTEIN II
Music by RICHARD RODGERS
Copyright © 1959 by Richard Rodgers and Oscar Hammerstein II
Copyright Renewed
WILLIAMSON MUSIC owner of publication and allied rights throughout the world
International Copyright Secured   All Rights Reserved

Bridge

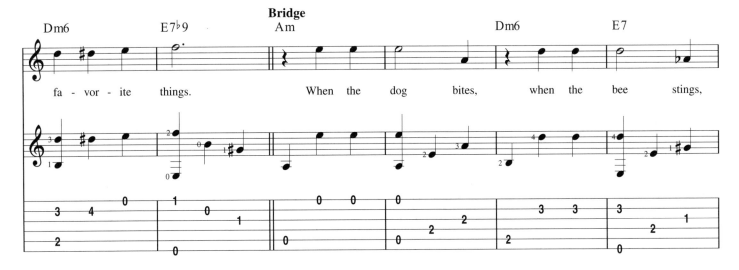

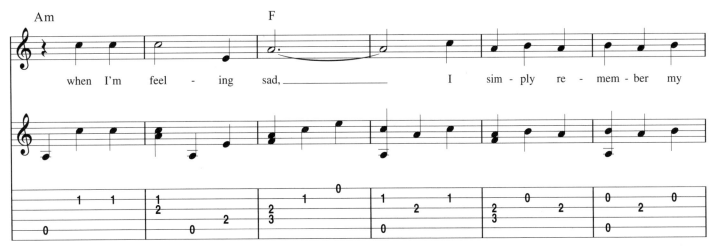

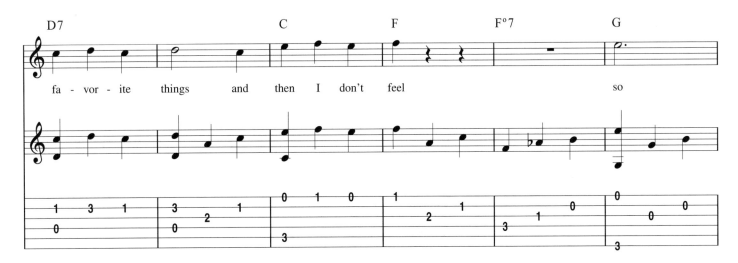

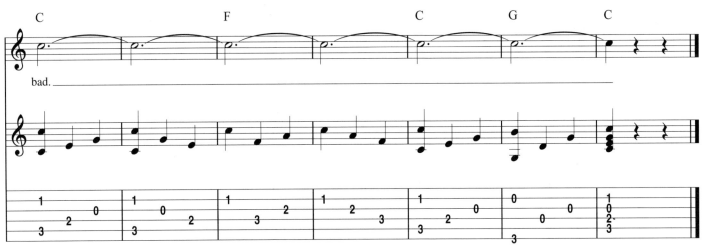

IMAGINE

Words and Music by JOHN LENNON

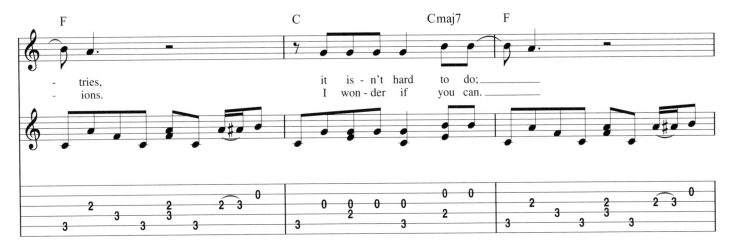

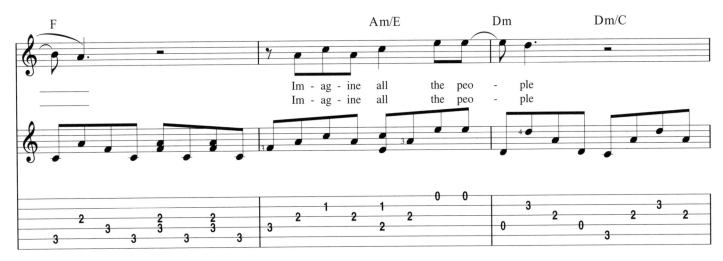

TRACK 73

Intro
Moderately ♩ = 138

Verse

1. How man - y roads must __ a man walk _____ down _____ be -
2. How many - y years can __ a mount - tain __ ex - ist _____ be -
3. How many - y times must __ a man look _____ up _____ be -

fore _____ you call him __ a man?
fore _____ it's washed to __ the sea?
fore _____ he can see __ the sky?

Chorus

an - swer, my friend,_____ is blow-in' in the wind._____ The

C   **D**   **G**   *Play 3 times*

an - swer___ is blow-in' in the wind.

Outro

The

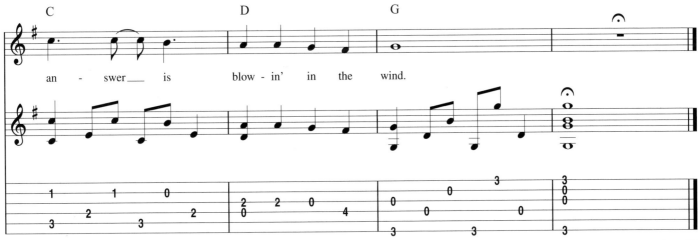

an - swer___ is blow-in' in the wind.

CHAPTER 5: USING A CAPO

Since the acoustic guitar is such a popular accompaniment instrument (either for yourself or other singers), it's essential that we address the use of a capo. This is not to say that non-singing guitarists don't have a need for them—far from it! But accompaniment is where the capo earns its living. Here are just a few instances when a capo can come in handy:

- **Avoiding the use of barre chords**: This is a big one, because let's face it—barre chords are simply no fun. With a capo, you can often find a way to play the same chords without having to barre at all.

- **Adjusting the key of a song to fit vocal range**: If you've ever tried singing a song that was just out of your reach, you can easily slap a capo onto the fretboard and transpose the song to a suitable key without having to relearn the guitar part.

- **Unplayable voicings**: Players sometimes use capos to access chord voicings that aren't otherwise playable.

WHAT IS A CAPO?

A capo is a mechanical device that clamps onto the neck of a guitar, barring across the strings at whichever fret you choose. In essence, it becomes a moveable nut, allowing you to raise the pitches of all six open strings evenly without having to retune the guitar. There are a few different types of capos available, with the most popular being the "quick-change" type. A "poor man's" capo can even be fashioned from a rubber band and a pen or pencil, if you're flat broke! Hopefully you won't have to resort to this, however, as you can usually purchase a perfectly decent capo for around $10.

Shubb "Original" Capo   Kyser "Quick Change" Capo

So how exactly do you use a capo? Let's learn how by examining each of the three instances described above.

Avoiding Barre Chords

Let's say the keyboardist in your band writes a new song in B♭ (as keyboardists love to do). He tells you he wants to have an acoustic guitar fingerpicking the chords for the verse. The chords are B♭, E♭, Gm, and Cm. Well, the capo-less guitarist may say "Yuck! All barre chords! Hello, finger cramps." The crafty guitarist, however, will say "No problem! Let me just slap a capo on fret 3 and I'll be ready to go."

Let's take a closer look at this progression. First, here's how you might be forced to play these chords without a capo.

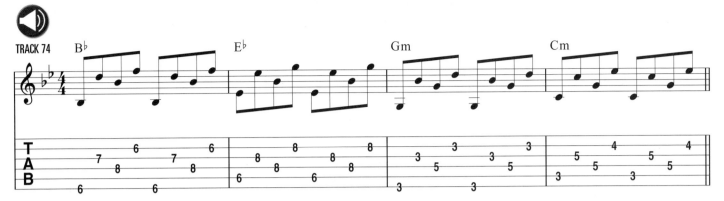

And here you can see how easily this progression can be played using a capo on fret 3. No more barre chords!

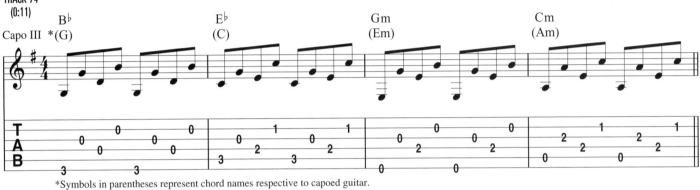

*Symbols in parentheses represent chord names respective to capoed guitar.
Symbols above reflect actual sounding chord. Capoed fret is "0" in tab.

Adjusting the Key for a Better Vocal Range

OK, say you've spent a lot of time learning to play your favorite country song, in the key of E. It's composed of I, IV, and V chords (E, A7, and B7), and you've even learned the little chordal embellishments. So now you're ready to sing along, and it's all going great when, whoa! You try your best to hit the low notes, but it ends up sounding more like a frog's croak. You have to transpose the song. You decide you need to bring it up a minor 3rd (to G) for it to be in a comfortable range. After playing the song with G, C7, and D7 shapes, you notice it just doesn't sound the same as it did in E. What to do? Simply slap a capo on the third fret, and you're able to play it the way you learned it with the E, A7, and B7 shapes and their attendant embellishments.

*Symbols in parentheses represent chord names respective to capoed guitar.
Symbols above reflect actual sounding chord. Capoed fret is "0" in tab.

A capo is also the perfect solution when you need to accompany a singer who's used to doing a song in a different key. Let's say, for example, you're doing a solo gig, and an audience member says, "Hey, you've gotta let my friend sing a song. She's really good! Please??!!!" Knowing that an extra tip may be in it for you, you oblige. Her friend comes up and says, "How about 'Yesterday' by the Beatles?" "No problem," you think. "In A♭," she says. You think, "Uh oh … I know it in G." Then you remember your trusty friend, the capo. You slap it onto the first fret and say, "Whenever you're ready."

YESTERDAY

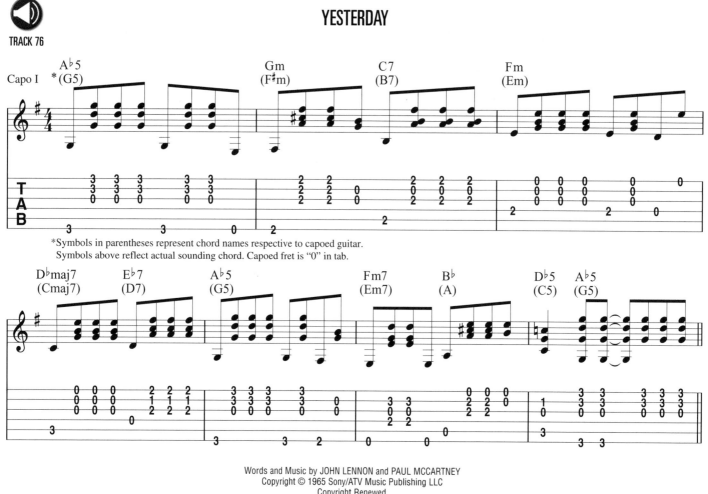

*Symbols in parentheses represent chord names respective to capoed guitar.
 Symbols above reflect actual sounding chord. Capoed fret is "0" in tab.

Unplayable Voicings

Let's say you're working on a solo piece in G minor, and the melody you hear in your head is G–A–B♭–D, with the notes all ringing together. You try fingering it all different kinds of ways, but none sounds right; there's just no way to do that on the guitar in that key. Or is there? With a capo on fret 3, to handle the B♭ and D notes for you, it suddenly becomes possible.

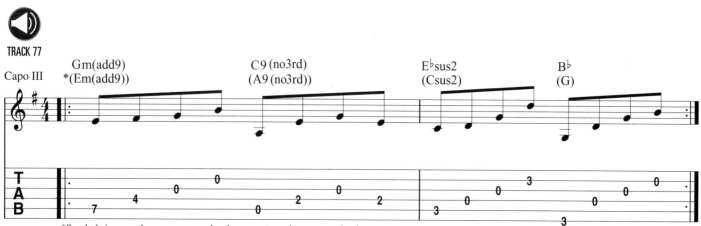

*Symbols in parentheses represent chord names respective to capoed guitar.
 Symbols above reflect actual sounding chord. Capoed fret is "0" in tab.

Let's take a look at some classic capoed riffs, all of which fall into one of the three mentioned instances for using a capo.

LANDSLIDE

TRACK 78

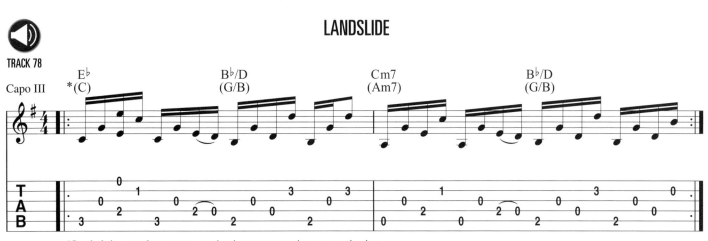

*Symbols in parentheses represent chord names respective to capoed guitar.
Symbols above reflect actual sounding chord. Capoed fret is "0" in tab.

IF I WROTE YOU

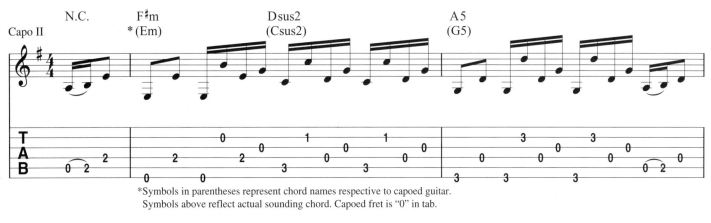

*Symbols in parentheses represent chord names respective to capoed guitar.
Symbols above reflect actual sounding chord. Capoed fret is "0" in tab.

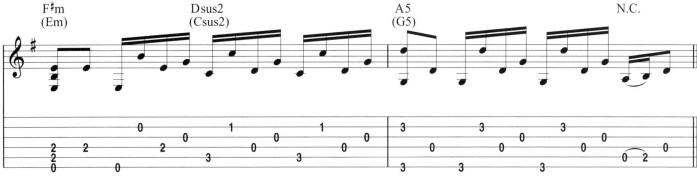

FIRE AND RAIN

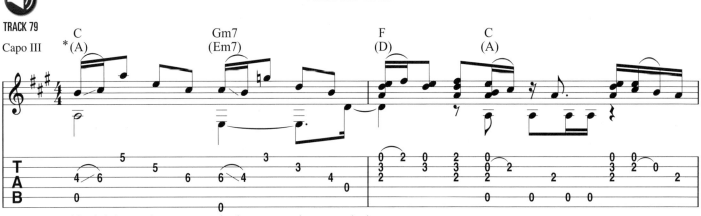

*Symbols in parentheses represent chord names respective to capoed guitar.
Symbols above reflect actual sounding chord. Capoed fret is "0" in tab.

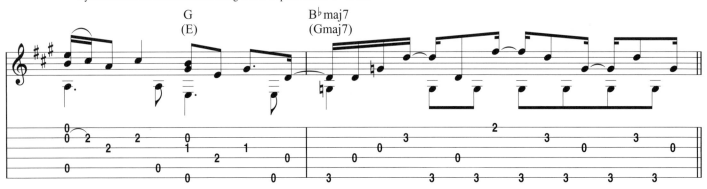

Words and Music by JAMES TAYLOR

LEADER OF THE BAND

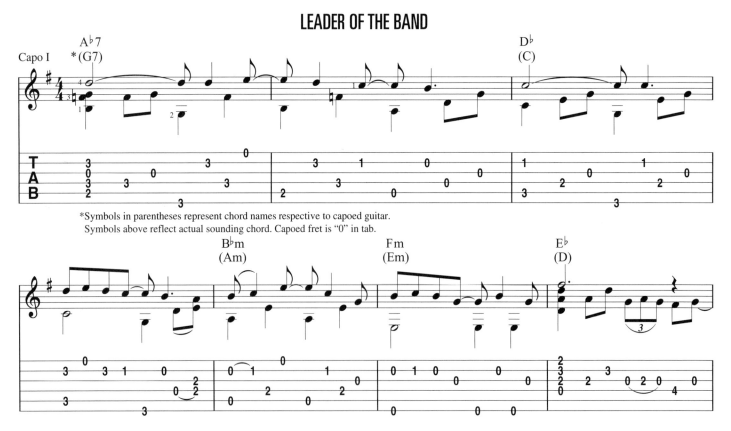

*Symbols in parentheses represent chord names respective to capoed guitar.
Symbols above reflect actual sounding chord. Capoed fret is "0" in tab.

Words and Music by DAN FOGELBERG

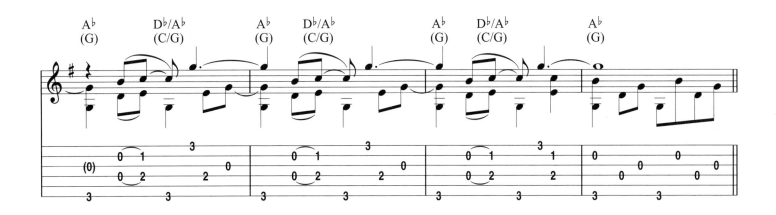

MICHELLE

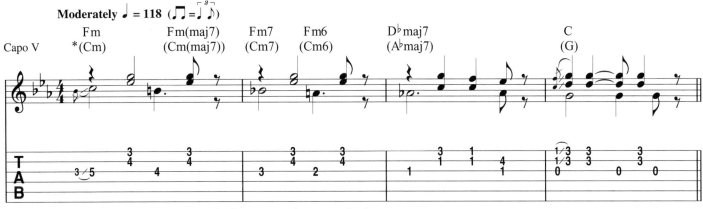

*Symbols in parentheses represent chord names respective to capoed guitar.
Symbols above reflect actual sounding chord. Capoed fret is "0" in tab.

Words and Music by JOHN LENNON and PAUL McCARTNEY
Copyright © 1965 Sony/ATV Music Publishing LLC
Copyright Renewed
All Rights Administered by Sony/ATV Music Publishing LLC, 8 Music Square West, Nashville, TN 37203
International Copyright Secured   All Rights Reserved

LEAST COMPLICATED

Words and Music by EMILY SALIERS
© 1994 EMI VIRGIN SONGS, INC. and GODHAP MUSIC
All Rights Controlled and Administered by EMI VIRGIN SONGS, INC.
All Rights Reserved   International Copyright Secured   Used by Permission

CHAPTER 6: ALTERNATE TUNINGS

Technically, an alternate tuning is created whenever one or more strings of the guitar are tuned to notes that differ from standard tuning (E–A–D–G–B–E). One of the most immediate benefits of an alternate tuning is the fresh perspective that it brings to the guitar. If you've never experimented with anything other than standard tuning, you'll likely be pleasantly surprised by the opportunities for new sounds that alternate tunings can afford. They're especially effective for getting out of a creative rut—a situation all too familiar to guitarists.

Alternate guitar tunings have a rich and diverse history. The great bluesmen of the thirties and forties made extensive use of numerous tunings, particularly open ones. In the seventies and eighties, solo fingerstyle virtuosos such as Michael Hedges and Leo Kottke brought D–A–D–G–A–D and other altered tunings to new audiences. There has even been recent growth in the popularity of alternate tunings in the rock guitar world. Still, acoustic fingerstyle guitar sees most of the action. Let's examine a few of the most common alternate tunings and see what they have to offer.

OPEN G

From the bluesmen of the Delta to the Rolling Stones, open G tuning (low to high, D–G–D–G–B–D) has seen plenty of action over the years. It not only allows you to play a chord (G major) with absolutely no fretting but also facilitates the easy, one-finger moveable barre chord. Here's how to access open G tuning, from standard tuning:

- Tune your sixth string down one whole step to match the pitch of your open D string.

- Tune your fifth string down one whole step to match the pitch of your open G string.

- Now tune your first string down one whole step to match the pitch of your open D string.

That's it—you're in open G.

Let's take a look at some fresh-sounding chord shapes in this tuning's home key of G. Notice how the standard I, IV, and V chords sound fresh and alive again in this tuning.

TRACK 80

In this next example, we're just moving a single chord shape up and down the neck while allowing the open first and second strings to drone. Listen to the full-sounding chords that result.

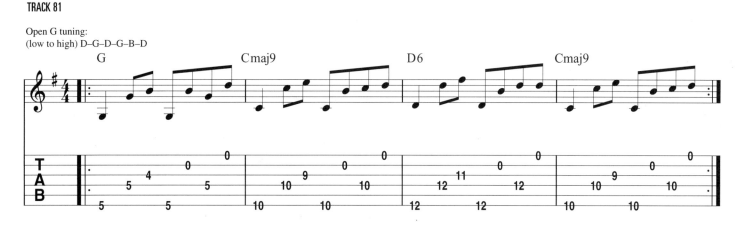

Open G tuning:
(low to high) D–G–D–G–B–D

While discovering all-new chord shapes is half the fun of using alternate tunings, here are several voicings each for I, IV, and V chords in the key of G. Try them in different combinations with several fingerpicking patterns and see what you come up with.

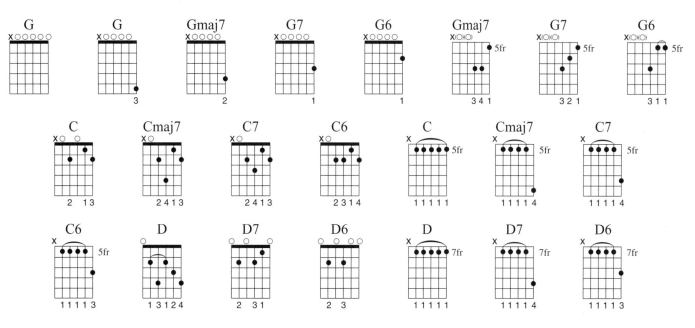

Now let's take a look at some classic riffs that make use of open G. First up is this classic turnaround lick from the intro to Robert Johnson's "Cross Road Blues." Consider this one a must-know blues lick in open G.

CROSS ROAD BLUES
(CROSSROADS)

Open G tuning:
(low to high) D–G–D–G–B–D

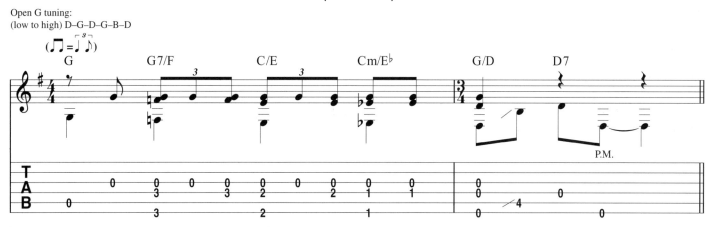

Words and Music by ROBERT JOHNSON
Copyright © (1978), 1990, 1991 MPCA King Of Spades (SESAC) and Claud L. Johnson
Administered by Music & Media International, Inc.
International Copyright Secured   All Rights Reserved

Notice how Leo Kottke makes use of half-step bends in "Machine 3" (a.k.a. "Vaseline Machine Gun") to spice up what is basically a variation on the Travis picking pattern.

MACHINE 3

Open G tuning:
(low to high) D–G–D–G–B–D

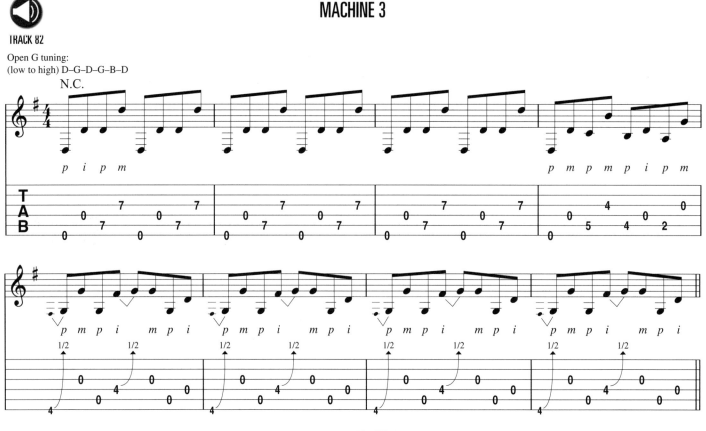

DROP D

Another extremely common alternate tuning is drop D (low to high, D–A–D–G–B–E). This tuning allows you to access octaves on strings 6 and 4 while keeping the rest of the guitar tuned in standard. In the realm of the acoustic guitar, drop D is often exploited in the solo guitar genre, as it allows the thumb to drone on the open D strings while playing chords and melodies on top. (Open G tuning allows octave drones as well—Ds on strings 6 and 4 and Gs on strings 5 and 3—and it's also commonly employed in similar fashion.) The only thing you need to do in order to reach drop D from standard tuning is lower your sixth string down a whole step to match your open D string. (If you're still in open G tuning, just bring your fifth and first strings back up a whole step and you're there.)

This Travis picking example exploits the octave D strings while moving an open D major chord shape up and down the fretboard.

Drop D tuning:
(low to high) D–A–D–G–B–E

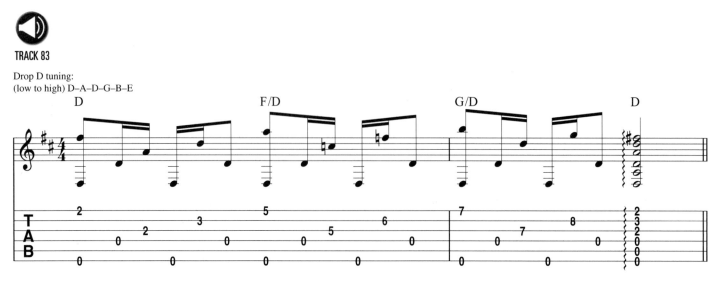

Here's another drop D example, this time embellished with a few hammer-ons.

TRACK 83
(0:13)

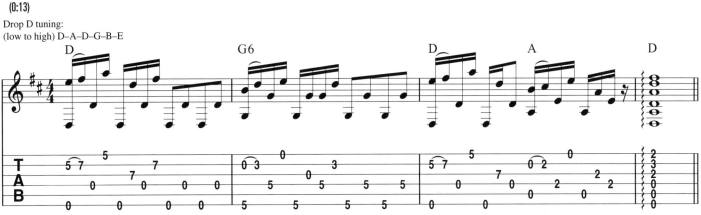

Drone/Melody Approach

A favorite device of acoustic fingerstyle guitarists is to combine a melodic approach with droning open strings. Notice that the first example here is actually from Chapter 3 (Right Hand Independence), except now we're alternating the low sixth-string D with the fourth-string D, resulting in a fuller sound.

TRACK 84

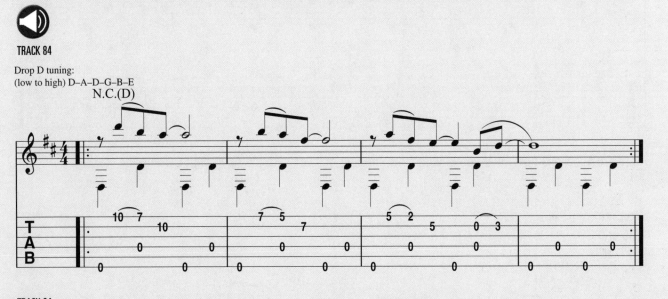

TRACK 84
(0:23)

These next two examples employ string-bending for a different sort of angle on drop D tuning and drones.

Drop D tuning:
(low to high) D–A–D–G–B–E

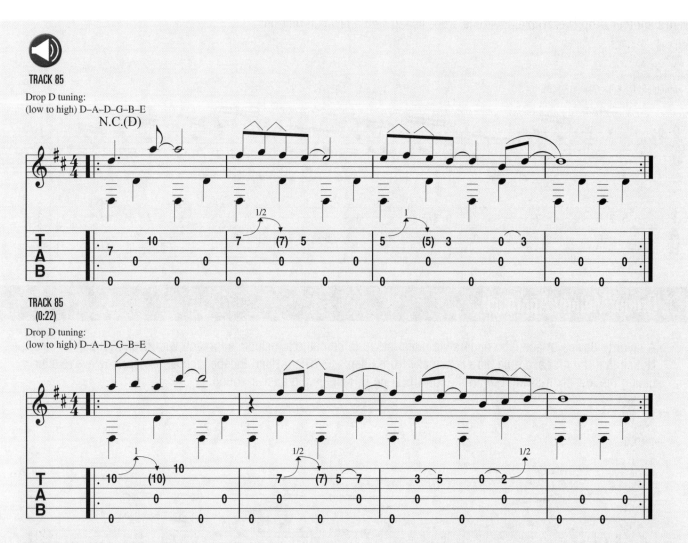

Drop D tuning:
(low to high) D–A–D–G–B–E

Here are a few examples that combine the low, droning octaves with the open high E string for maximum ringing effect.

Drop D tuning:
(low to high) D–A–D–G–B–E

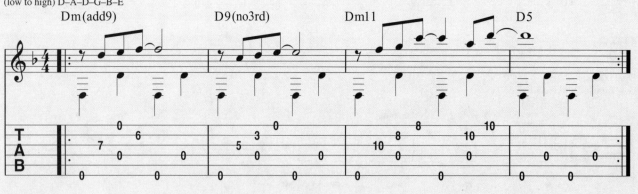

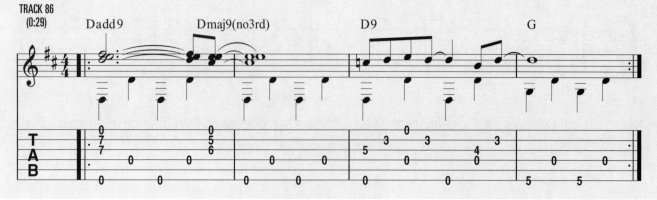

Now let's check out some pop songs that put drop D tuning to use.

DEAR PRUDENCE

Drop D tuning:
(low to high) D–A–D–G–B–E

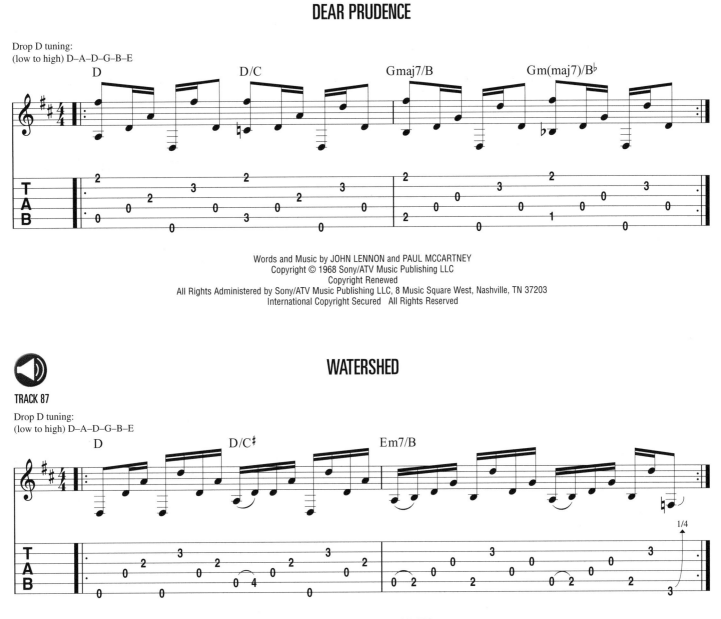

WATERSHED

TRACK 87

Drop D tuning:
(low to high) D–A–D–G–B–E

Following are two more riffs from different tunings thrown in for good measure. First, Dar Williams uses a variation on open G tuning for "When I Was a Boy," where the B string is tuned down to A. Then David Wilcox makes use of D–A–D–G–A–D tuning for "Radio Men." Notice that these two tunings differ only in the fifth string.

WHEN I WAS A BOY

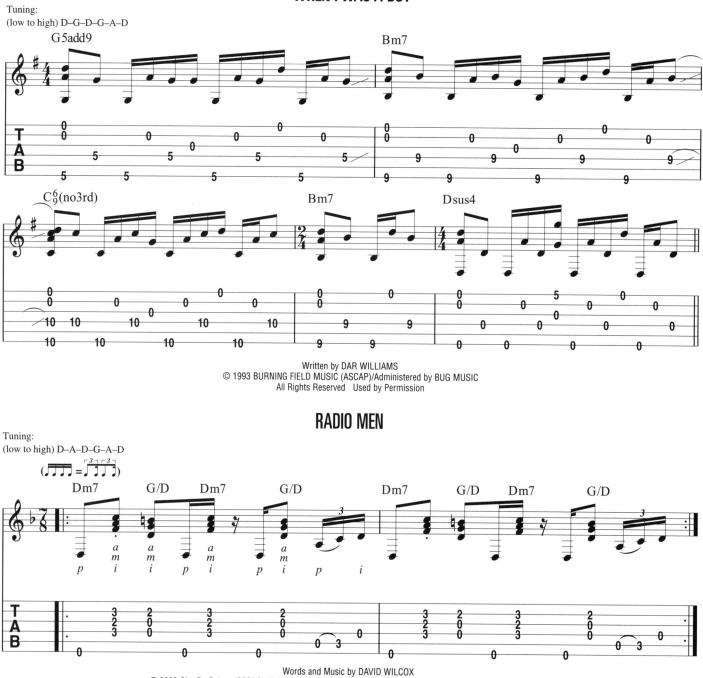

RADIO MEN

Other Alternate Tunings

Here is a list of some additional alternate tunings for you to explore. This is by no means comprehensive, but it's a good start. Feel free to add to this list by altering a string or two from one of these tunings. Experiment! Many times a new tuning can inspire a whole song.

Double Drop D (D–A–D–G–B–D)

Dsus4 (D–A–D–G–A–D) (Typically referred to as "Dadgad")

Open D (D–A–D–F♯–A–D)

Open Gm (D–G–D–G–B♭–D)

Open A (E–A–E–A–C♯–E)

Open E (E–B–E–G♯–B–E)

Open Em (E–B–E–G–B–E)

Open C (C–G–C–G–C–E)

We'll visit alternate tunings again in the final two chapters, as they're extremely common in solo guitar arrangements.

CHAPTER 7: ARRANGING FOR SOLO GUITAR—PART 2

In this chapter we apply the concepts we've already covered (capos, alternate tunings, and so forth) to some slightly more advanced song arrangements. Along the way, we'll also explore some new fingerstyle techniques to further develop your skills.

COME TOGETHER

Double Drop D Tuning: low to high (D–A–D–G–B–D)

Our first advanced arrangement will be the Beatles' "Come Together." Make sure to tune your guitar to double drop D tuning, as noted above. This arrangement introduces two new technical concepts: the *thumb plectrum style* and *string stopping*. Let's take a look at each of these and how they apply to this song.

Thumb Plectrum Style

This technique involves "strumming" more than one string at a time with the thumb. This usually includes two or three notes, but it occasionally involves all six strings. In "Come Together," you'll strike the lowest two strings at the same time, to mimic the "boogie-woogie" rhythm that supports the song's verses. Many players find this technique much easier to execute using a thumbpick. You might want to experiment with both methods to see which suits you. Here's a look at the main verse figure, as adapted for solo guitar.

TRACK 88

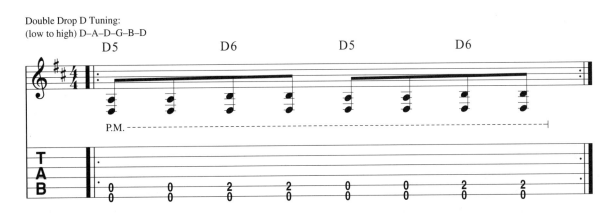

Notice that the tuning allows this riff to be played with only one fretting finger, therefore freeing up your other fingers for melody notes on top (which we'll see in the actual arrangement). For authenticity, palm mute the bass strings by allowing your right palm to lightly touch the strings near the bridge. This is a big part of the sound and also helps to separate the bass strings from the treble strings, thereby reinforcing the illusion of two distinct instruments.

Here's the second boogie-woogie pattern in "Come Together"—this time for the A chord.

TRACK 88
(0:11)

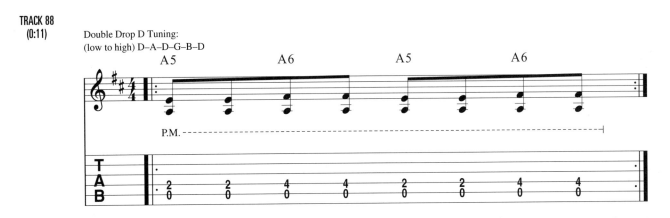

For the last part of the verse, we strum through all six strings with the thumb for a dramatic effect on the G7 chord:

String Stopping

Occasionally in solo guitar arrangements, an open-string melody note is followed by another melody note on a different string. See the example below:

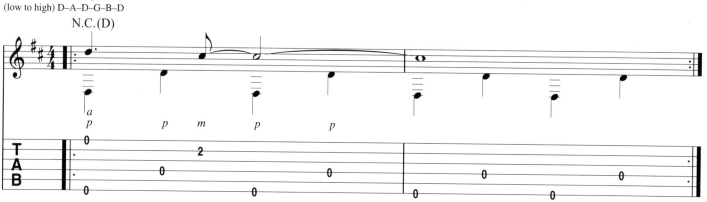

This can sound very nice in some instances, but sometimes you might not want all the notes to ring together. String stopping to the rescue! With this technique, your right-hand fingers will not only strike the strings at the appropriate time, they will also mute them when needed. In this case, the first D note in the melody rubs against the following C♯ note. Since this D is an open string, the only way to stop it is with your right hand. So, the *a* finger (as indicated between the notation and tab staves) will simultaneously plant onto that first string as the *m* finger strikes the C♯ note. The result is a clearly articulated melody with no extraneous ringing.

Another instance when string stopping comes in handy is when you're barring a chord with two melody notes on two different strings. For instance, in the chorus of "Come Together," while barring at the seventh fret for the Bm7 chord, the melody goes from A on string 1 to F# on string 2. Because the same fret-hand finger is barring both notes, you need to stop the first string with the right hand's *a* finger.

TRACK 89
(0:26)

Double Drop D Tuning:
(low to high) D–A–D–G–B–D

Now let's take a look at the complete arrangement of "Come Together." Before digging in, however, let's examine a few noteworthy elements:

- The interlude following the chorus is essentially a repeat of the intro, but the top notes are harmonized. This is a nice way to give your arrangements a sense of direction.

- For the A chord in the verse, the melody is entirely on the B string, even though the E note could be played on the first string by barring the first finger across fret 2. The reason for this is to avoid any incidental sounding of the C# note at fret 2 of the B string.

- Make sure the E–D–B pull-off in the chorus sounds clearly. Your right hand independence will be tested there!

If you find any other trouble spots, work up the parts individually and slowly before attempting to put them together. And most importantly, have fun!

TRACK 90

COME TOGETHER

Double Drop D Tuning:
(low to high) D–A–D–G–B–D

Slow Rock ♩ = 76
Intro
N.C.(Dm7)

TEARS IN HEAVEN

Open G Tuning: (low to high) D–G–D–G–B–D, Capo II

Our second arrangement will be Eric Clapton's "Tears in Heaven." Arranged in open G tuning with a capo at the second fret, the song still sounds in its original key of A. We'll encounter a few new concepts here as well: *countermelodies* and *octave transference*. Before taking on the whole arrangement, let's take a look at each of these new concepts and how they apply to this song.

Countermelodies

A countermelody can be thought of as a nice piece of "ear candy." It's simply another melody that's heard in conjunction with (or in the spaces between) the main melody. Their primary purpose is to add depth to your arrangements, as the listener may not notice them on the first few passes.

In solo guitar arrangements, countermelodies are often found in the bass, as in this example, where it fills the gaps of the main melody.

TRACK 91

Open G Tuning:
(low to high) D–G–D–G–B–D

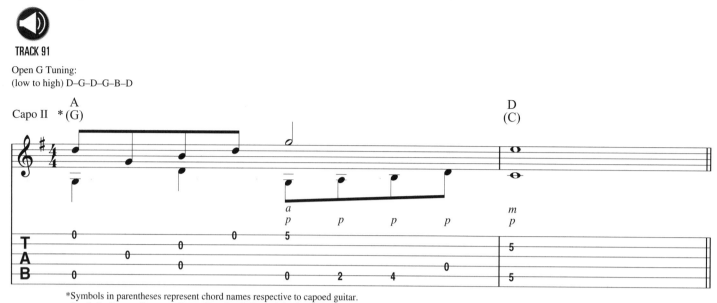

*Symbols in parentheses represent chord names respective to capoed guitar.
 Symbols above reflect actual sounding chord. Capoed fret is "0" in tab.

Sometimes a countermelody will appear against the main melody itself, as in this example.

TRACK 91
(0:11)

Open G Tuning:
(low to high) D–G–D–G–B–D

*Symbols in parentheses represent chord names respective to capoed guitar.
 Symbols above reflect actual sounding chord. Capoed fret is "0" in tab.

Here's how a countermelody can be used in the verses for "Tears in Heaven."

TRACK 91
(0:19)

Open G Tuning:
(low to high) D–G–D–G–B–D

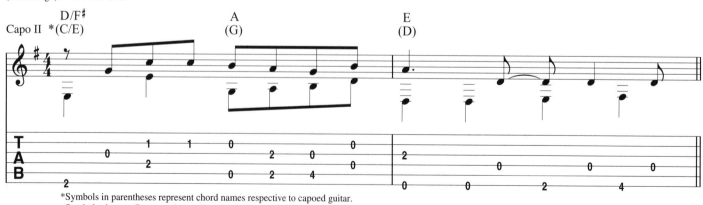

*Symbols in parentheses represent chord names respective to capoed guitar.
 Symbols above reflect actual sounding chord. Capoed fret is "0" in tab.

Octave Transference

Sometimes you might want to provide an additional level of interest when repeating a melody. This can be especially effective in solo arrangements, where you don't have different lyrics to bring a repeated melody to life. In these instances, try transferring the melody up one octave, to make it sound fresh and new. Of course, this will sometimes mean a bit of experimenting with the bass and accompaniment in order to support the new register. But it's well worth the effort.

Let's take a closer look at octave transference. Here we have a standard, repeated melody.

TRACK 92

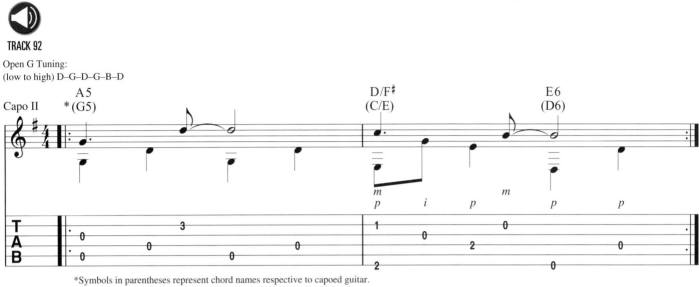

*Symbols in parentheses represent chord names respective to capoed guitar.
Symbols above reflect actual sounding chord. Capoed fret is "0" in tab.

Now let's transfer the melody up an octave on the repeat. Notice the use of a natural harmonic to provide extra color. We've also replaced the standard C/E harmony with a Cmaj7/E.

TRACK 92
(0:17)

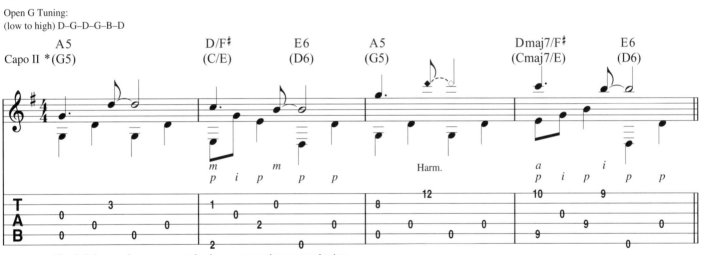

*Symbols in parentheses represent chord names respective to capoed guitar.
Symbols above reflect actual sounding chord. Capoed fret is "0" in tab.

Our arrangement of "Tears in Heaven" uses octave transference in the verses as well.

TRACK 92
(0:31)

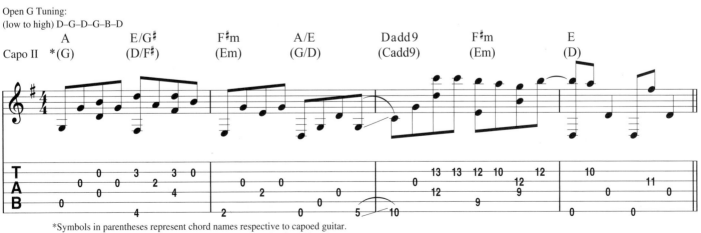

*Symbols in parentheses represent chord names respective to capoed guitar.
Symbols above reflect actual sounding chord. Capoed fret is "0" in tab.

Now let's play through the entire arrangement. Watch for the following elements:

- The melody moves up an octave during the last part of the verse and doesn't come back down until the very last line of the chorus.

- The verse melody is reharmonized in measure 11.

- As a contrast in texture, the bridge abandons the Travis picking thumb style and uses more of an arpeggiation style.

TEARS IN HEAVEN

TRACK 93

Words and Music by ERIC CLAPTON and WILL JENNINGS
Copyright © 1992 by E.C. Music Ltd. and Blue Sky Rider Songs
All Rights for E.C. Music Ltd. Administered by Unichappell Music Inc.
All Rights for Blue Sky Rider Songs Administered by Irving Music, Inc.
International Copyright Secured   All Rights Reserved

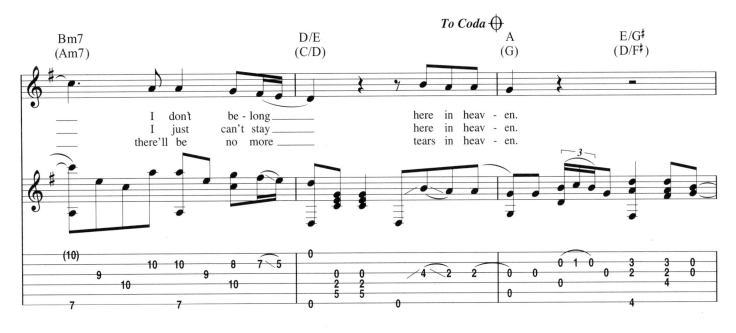

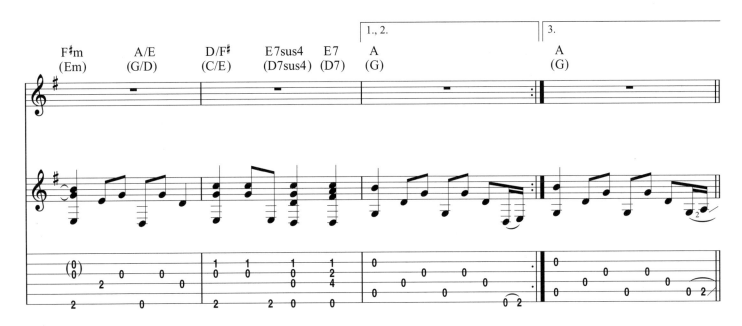

Time can bring you down, ___ time can bend your knees. ___

Time can break your heart, ___ have you beg - gin' please, ___ beg-gin' please.

Interlude

D.S. al Coda

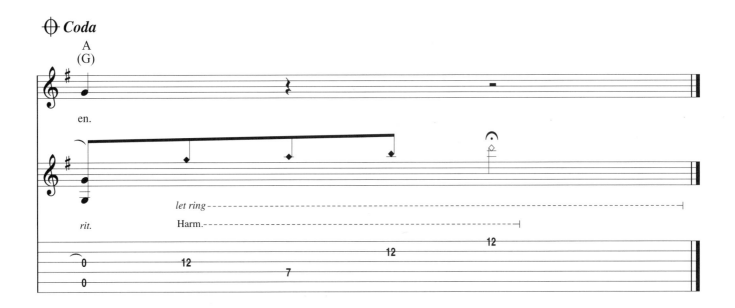

WHAT A WONDERFUL WORLD

Double Drop D Tuning: low to high (D–A–D–G–B–D)

The last advanced arrangement we're going to look at is Louis Armstrong's classic "What a Wonderful World." The guitar is in double drop D tuning, but the key is C major. In this arrangement we'll be using some jazzier harmonies and dividing the guitar part into three distinct parts: melody, chords, and bass. There are a few concepts in this arrangement worth further study as well: *melodic mixing of open and fretted notes*, and *alternate voicings and harmony*. Let's take a look at each of these and how they apply to this song.

Melodic Mixing of Open and Fretted Notes

In the "Come Together" arrangement earlier in this chapter, we learned about string stopping as a way to prevent certain melody notes from bleeding together. Now we're going to take a look at the opposite effect. Besides allowing you access to sometimes unplayable melody notes, mixing open strings with fretted notes also provides an interesting tonal color and the opportunity to ring several notes together for a harp-like effect. (Chet Atkins was a master at using this device.)

Let's take a look at an example. Here we have the melody E–D–C♯–B. In double drop D tuning, the top two open strings are D and B. Therefore, we can let those ring against fretted notes on different strings. Hold all fretted notes as long as possible, to achieve the maximum ringing effect.

TRACK 94

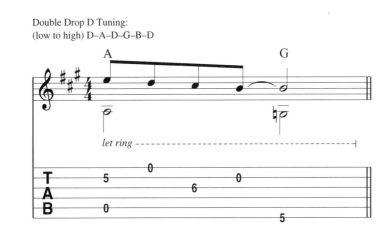

This same melody can also be played higher on the neck, allowing all four notes to ring together at once. (Notice that we're forced to transpose the bass note up an octave due to the higher position on the neck.)

TRACK 94
(0:08)

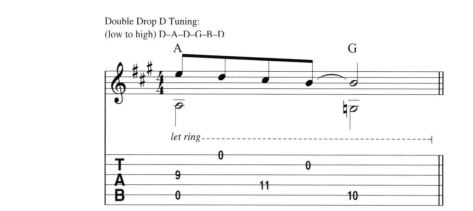

Here's how this technique is employed at the end of each verse in "What a Wonderful World."

TRACK 94
(0:12)

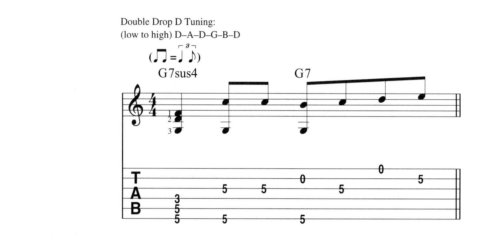

Alternate Voicings or Harmony

Often times in arrangements, a slight change in a chord voicing can add life to a repeated melodic phrase. This is especially true in instrumental arrangements, where we don't have the benefit of sung lyrics to help refresh a melody. In "What a Wonderful World," we use both *alternate voicings* (vertical reorganization of the same notes) and *alternate harmony* (different chords) to add interest during a repeated phrase.

Example A is from the first verse, while example B shows the same melody harmonized in verse 2. Notice that the Fadd9 has been replaced with Fmaj7, and the Em7 voicing is different.

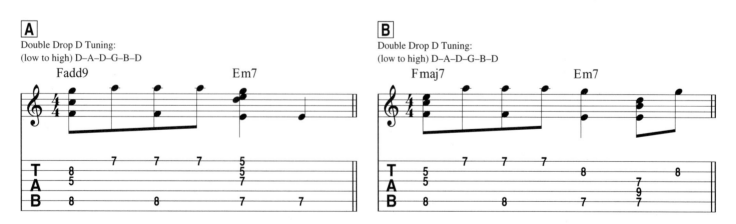

Here's another example of an alternate harmony. At the end of the second verse, the A♭maj7 from the first verse (example A) is replaced with the A♭add9 harmony (example B).

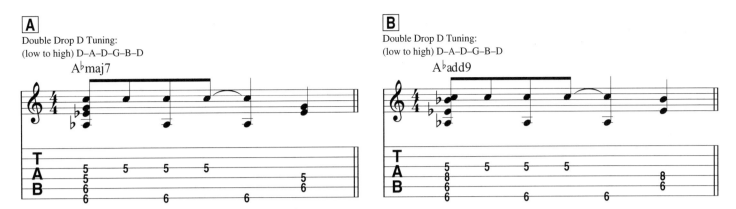

Now let's play through the whole arrangement of "What a Wonderful World." Watch for the following elements:

- The bass notes keep a steady quarter-note pulse throughout most of the piece, but the rhythm of the chords (mostly dyads on strings 3–5) is varied from section to section. This helps to maintain listener interest and the illusion of separate parts.

- Arpeggiation is used at the end of each verse to outline the chords for the turnaround. This varies the texture and helps keep things interesting.

- There are a few position shifts you'll need to make throughout. Take your time with these; you don't want them to sound abrupt. It's sort of a mind over matter issue. If you go into them with a hurried, anxious mind-set, it will likely sound that way. If you relax and imagine that you have all the time in the world, the result is usually much more musical. You don't want to interrupt the tempo of the song, but you do have a little liberty with it, since it's a solo arrangement.

WHAT A WONDERFUL WORLD

TRACK 95

Words and Music by GEORGE DAVID WEISS and BOB THIELE

Bridge

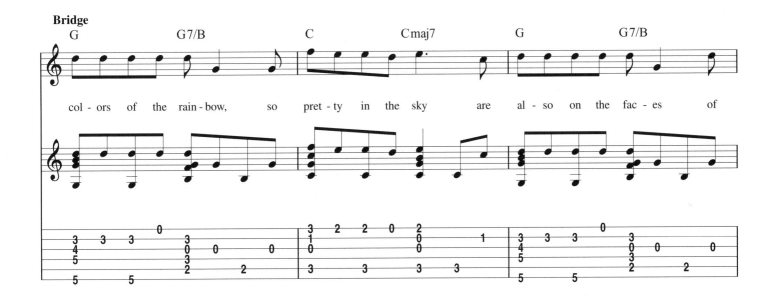

col - ors of the rain - bow, so pret - ty in the sky are al - so on the fac - es of

peo - ple go - in' by. ___ I see friends shak - in' hands ___ say - in',

D.S. al Coda

"How do you do?" ___ They're real - ly say - in' "I love you." 3. I hear

CHAPTER 8:
FOUR SOLO FINGERSTYLE SONGS

In this final chapter we're going to take a look at four complete transcriptions of pieces from masters in the fingerstyle genre. This will give you something to shoot for with the skills they've acquired thus far. These pieces will make use of most of the techniques we've looked at throughout the book, so if you've skipped any sections, now's your chance to go back and cram for this final fingerstyle test!

"LAST TRACK"

ADRIAN LEGG

Anyone who's familiar with Adrian Legg has probably heard of his innovative use of banjo-like tuners fitted with stops, allowing him to retune in the middle of songs with pinpoint accuracy. While he's dropped many, many jaws in his day, he's managed to compose a few pieces suitable for the intermediate fingerstylist as well. "Last Track" is, for the most part, the model Travis picking song. The thumb rocks back and forth throughout the entire song, allowing you to concentrate on the graceful melody. There aren't too many tricks up Adrian's sleeve on this one, so it shouldn't take too long to get under your fingers. Consequently, this is an ideal song with which to try the string-stopping technique we learned earlier. The song will have a different flavor depending on whether you allow all the melody notes to ring or make them distinct and precise with string stopping.

TRACK 96

LAST TRACK

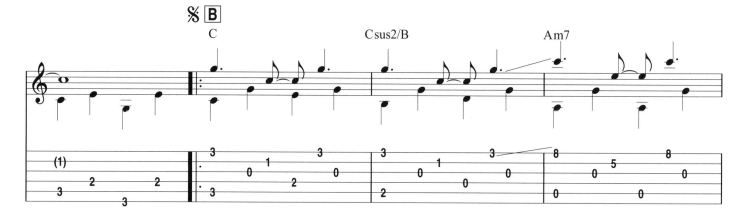

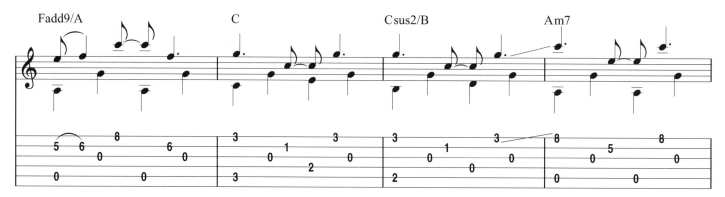

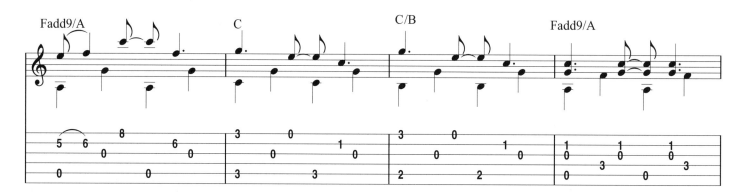

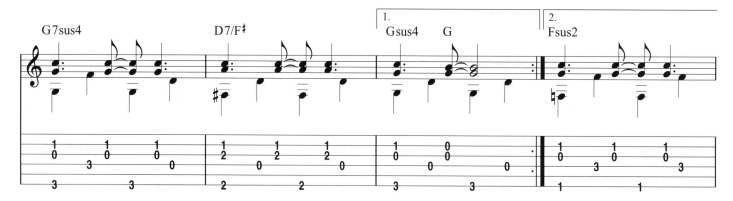

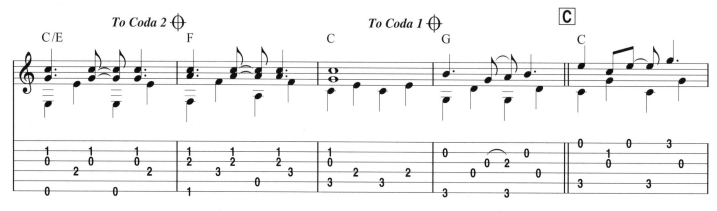

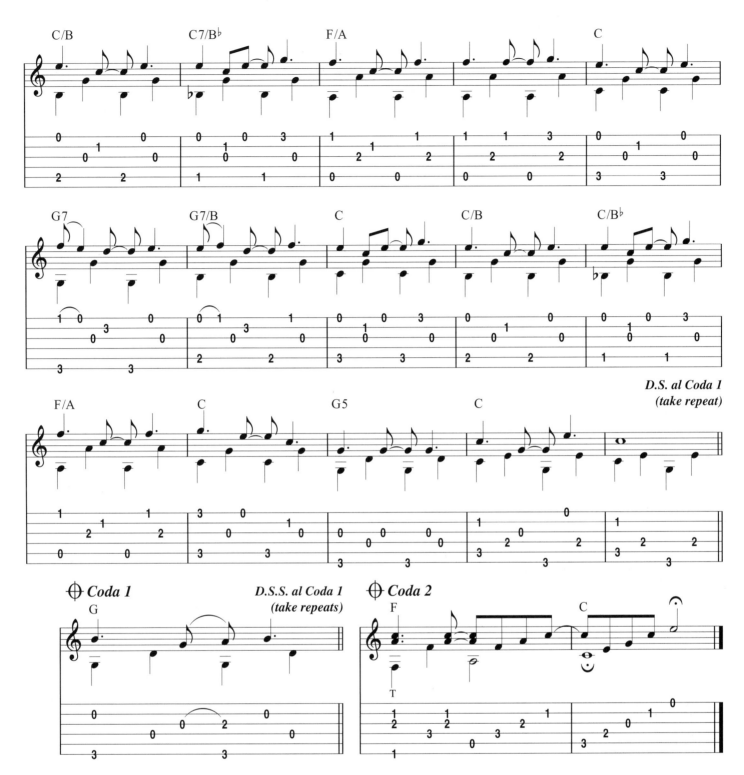

"JACK FIG"

LEO KOTTKE

"Jack Fig" is a short-and-sweet romp in open G tuning. In the original Leo Kottke recording, Leo is tuned down *two steps* from open G, resulting in a tuning of B♭–E♭–B♭–E♭–G–B♭, low to high. Considering this, you may want to use heavier gauged strings to avoid excessive flabbiness. This is especially a factor in this tune, as Leo really digs in and plays with serious conviction through most of the song. The song was recorded on a 12-string, as is common practice for Leo, but it sounds quite nice on a 6-string as well. For the purposes of this method, "Jack Fig" is played on a 6-string in regular open G tuning on the accompanying CD.

For much of the tune, your thumb will be pounding out the open fifth string while the other fingers handle melodies on the higher strings, but be sure to pay attention, as Leo will throw a monkey wrench into this method from time to time. Be sure to take notice of these specific technical challenges:

- You'll get plenty of practice moving your right hand to different string groups with this tune, as your *i* finger will need to cover the fourth or fifth strings at times, your *m* finger will cover the third or fourth strings, etc.

- In the sliding dyadic main theme, Leo frequently slides from two notes on different frets (such as 8 and 9) to two notes on the same fret (such as 12 and 12), or vice versa, sliding from two notes on the same fret (such as 7 and 7) to notes on different frets (such as 8 and 9). This requires a bit of fingertwisting, and care must be taken, especially when playing the song up to tempo. Use your index finger as a small barre to accommodate many of these dyads.

- Watch for the sneaky 7/8 measures thrown in from time to time.

- Notice that Leo's not afraid to abandon the standard thumping bass pattern at times in order to facilitate different melodies and textures, as in sections D and F.

JACK FIG

TRACK 97

Open G tuning:
(low to high) D–G–D–G–B–D

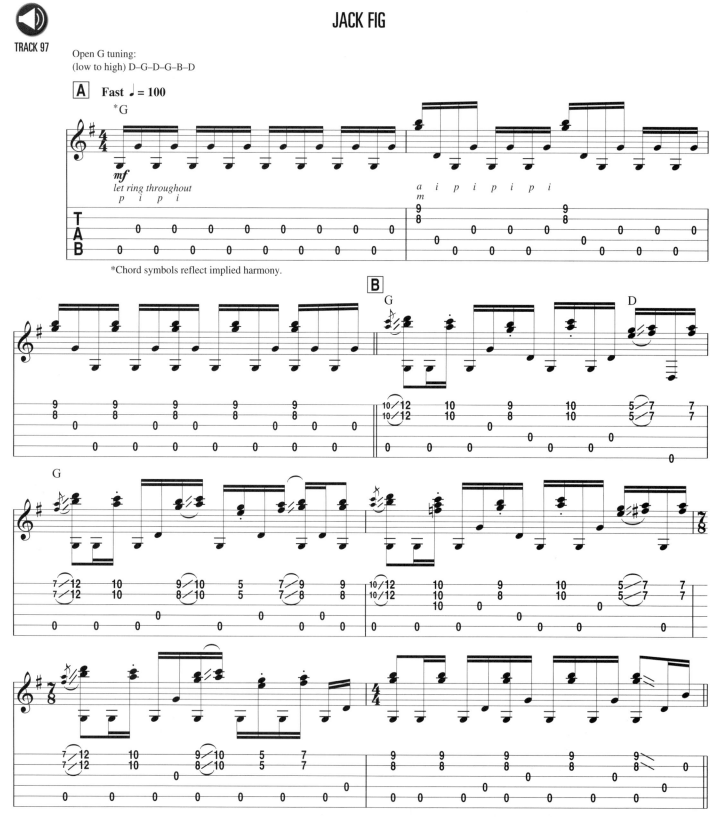

*Chord symbols reflect implied harmony.

By J.S. BACH
Arranged by Leo Kottke
© 1970 (Renewed 1998) OVERDRIVE MUSIC (ASCAP)/Administered by BUG MUSIC
All Rights Reserved   Used by Permission

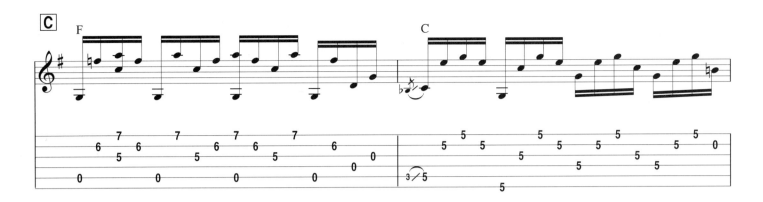

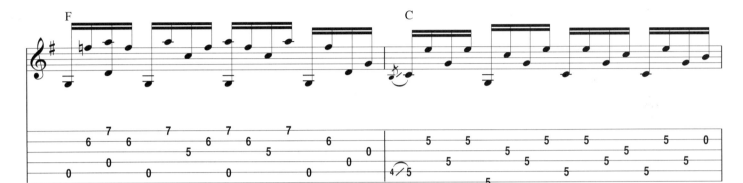

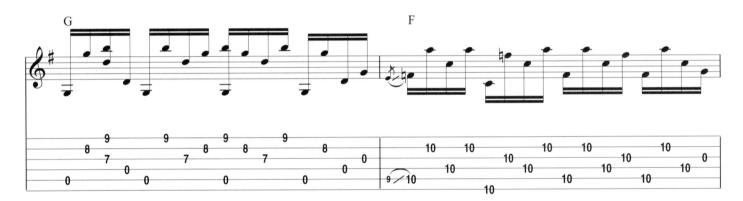

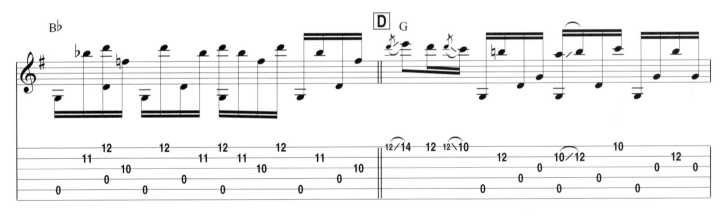

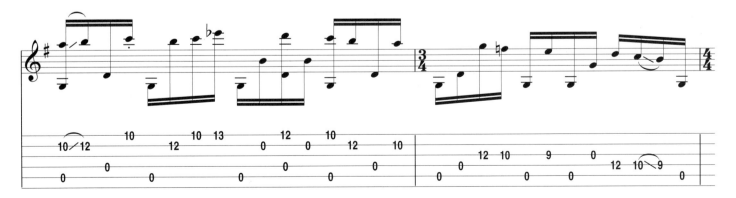

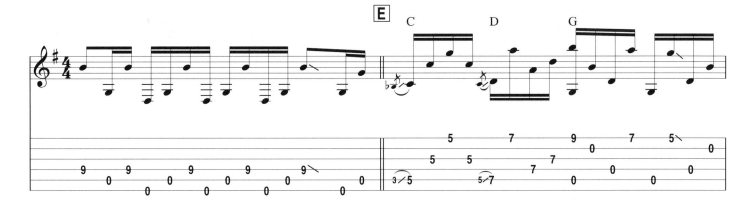

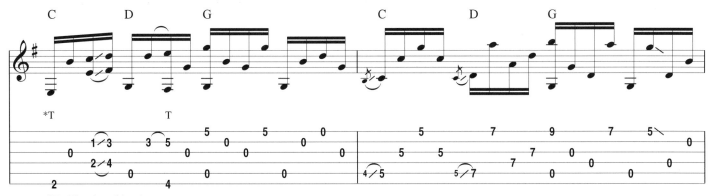

*T = Thumb on 6th string

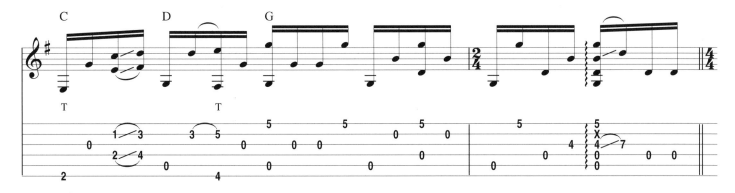

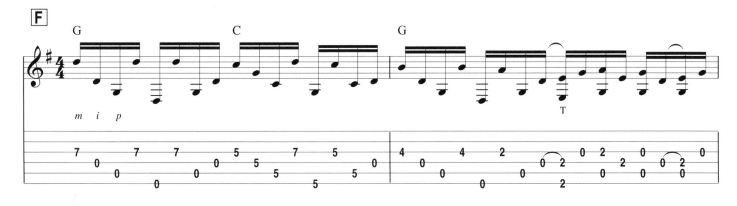

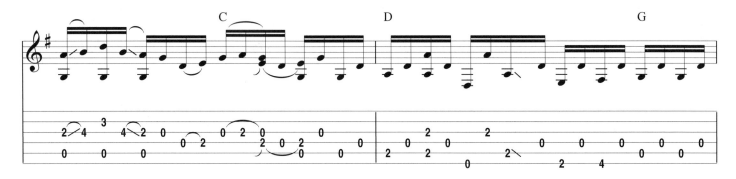

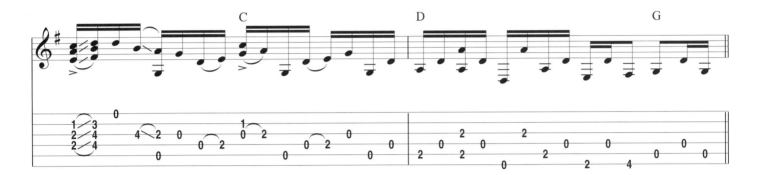

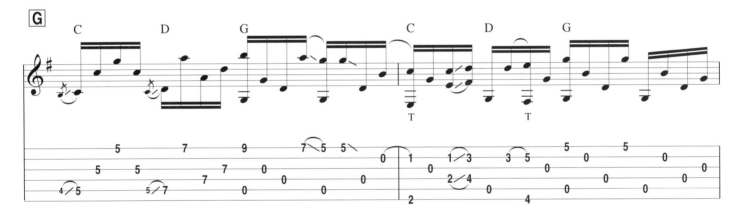

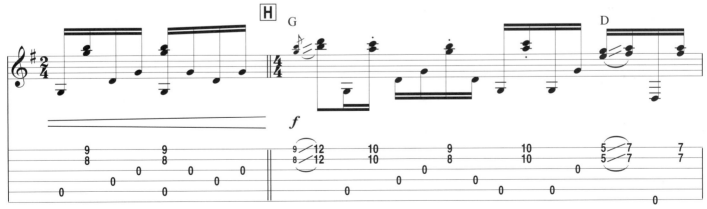

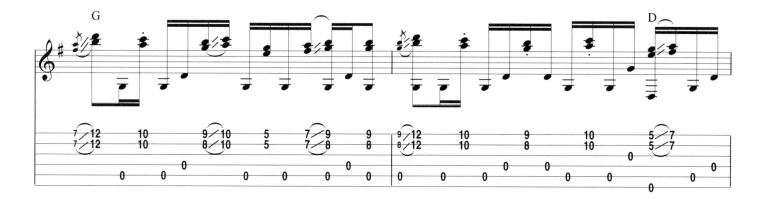

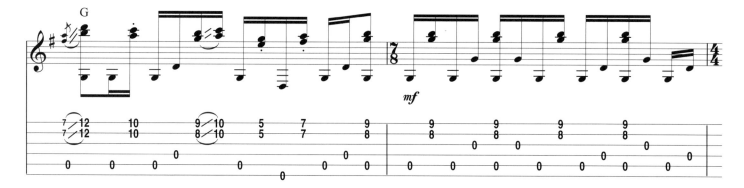

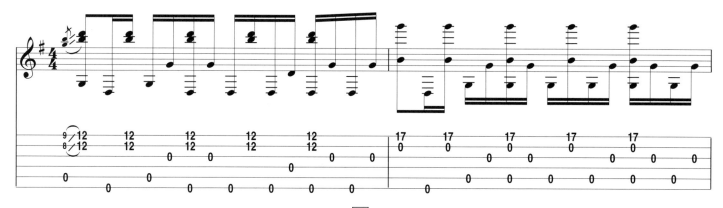

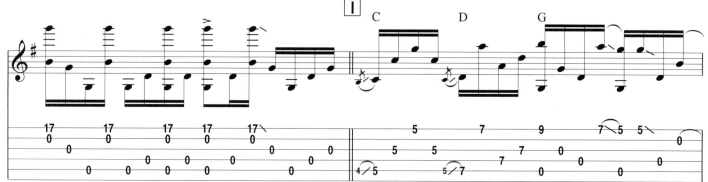

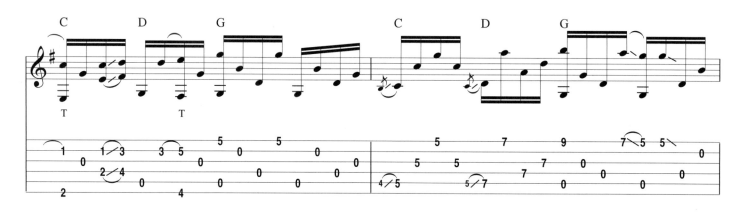

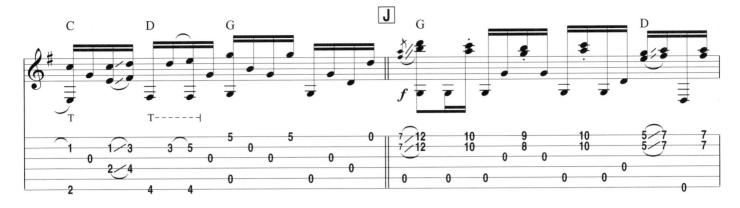

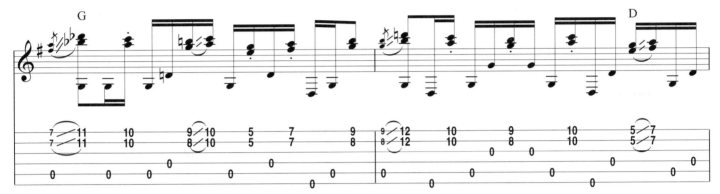

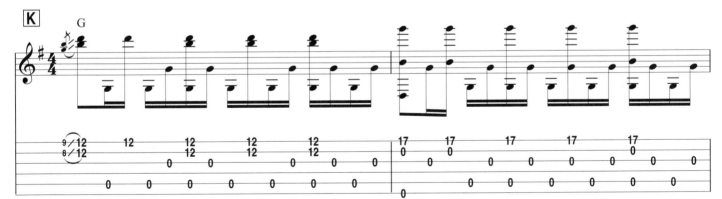

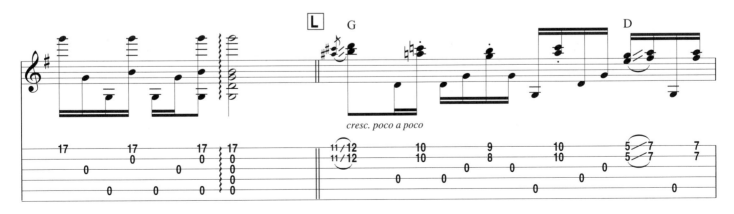

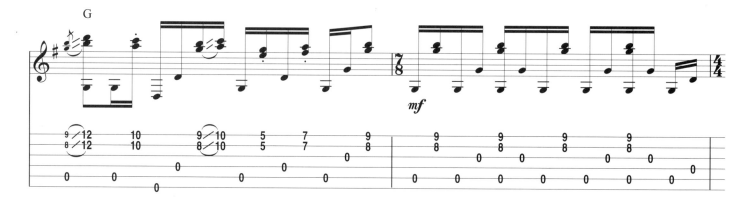

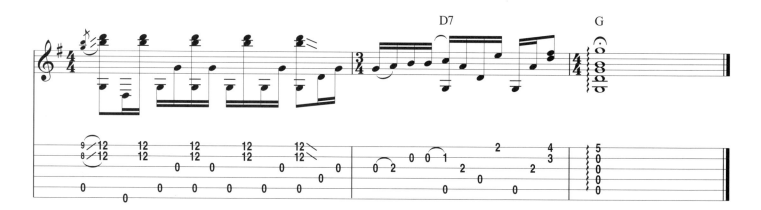

"SONG FOR GEORGE"

ERIC JOHNSON

Just about every guitarist is familiar with Eric Johnson's virtuosity on the electric guitar, but he's an extremely accomplished fingerstyle player as well. "Song for George," from his classic *Ah Via Musicom* album, is in double drop D tuning. The song is built upon the basic framework of an alternating thumb bass, but there's plenty of fancy melodic work thrown in as well, to spice things up. Take your time with this one, and pay attention to these specific elements:

- Johnson's use of quarter-step bends throughout lends a bluesy feel.

- Notice how he occasionally abandons the bass altogether (or sustains a single bass note) in order to facilitate more complex melody work. Timing is important in these instances, since you don't have the thumb pounding out steady eighth notes to hold things down.

- In the B section, the syncopated bass notes are not as difficult as they appear. They're actually serving more as interjections between the melody notes.

- The C section is deceptively difficult, because your thumb is having to work overtime. Take it slowly and work up the parts individually if necessary.

Once you've got the piece technically under your fingers, make sure and play it with attitude!

TRACK 98

Double Drop D Tuning:
(low to high) D–A–D–G–B–D

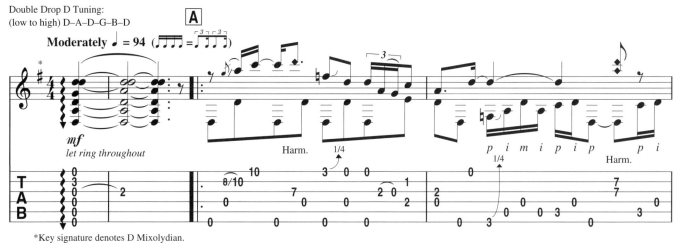

*Key signature denotes D Mixolydian.

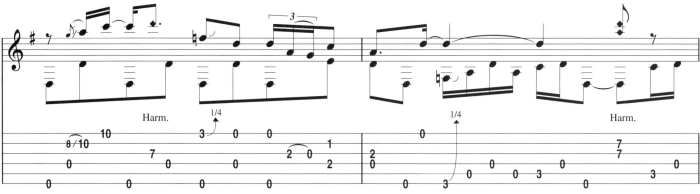

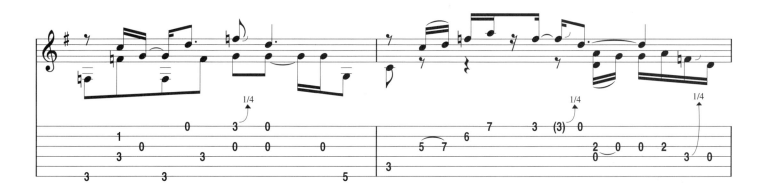

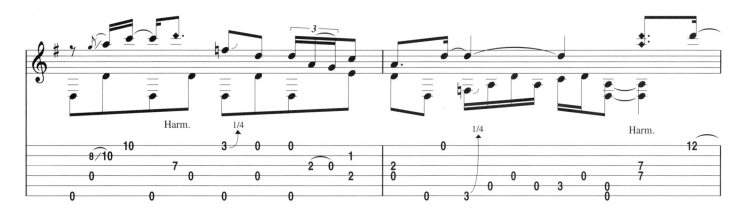

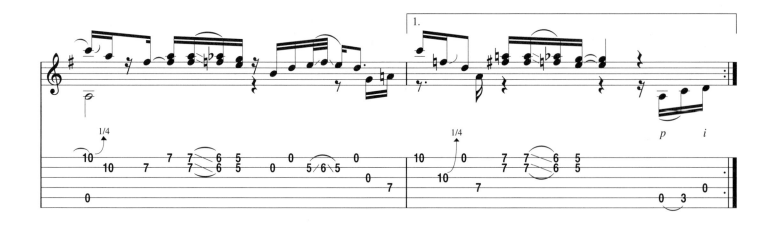

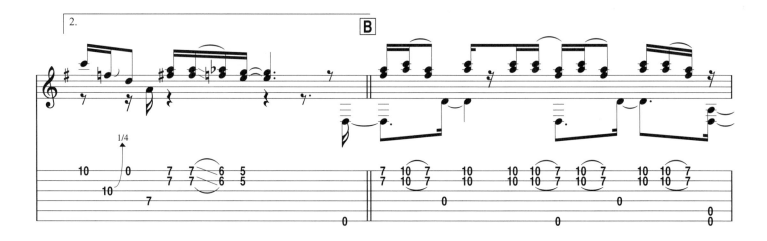

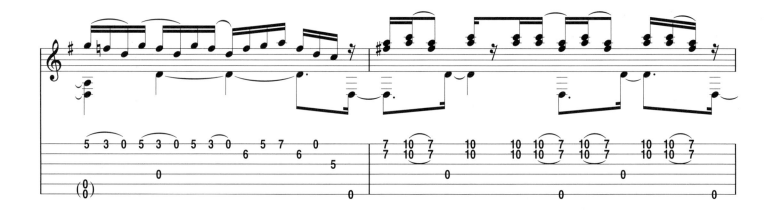

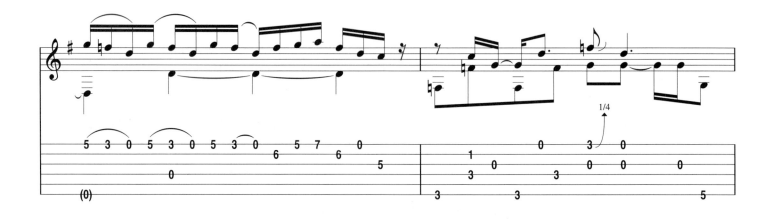

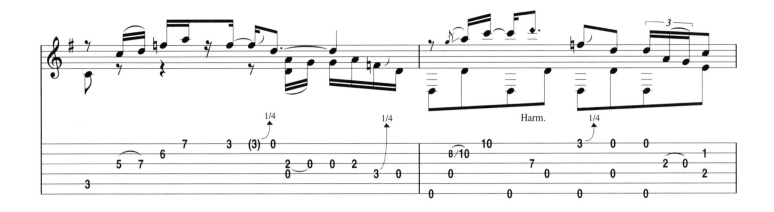

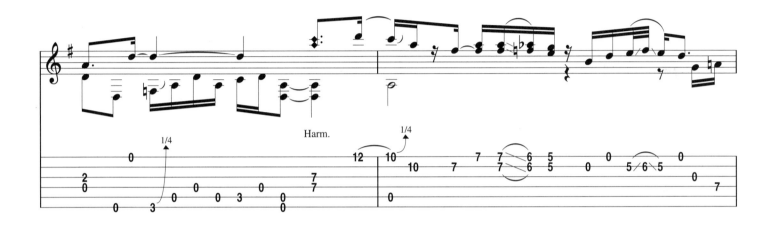

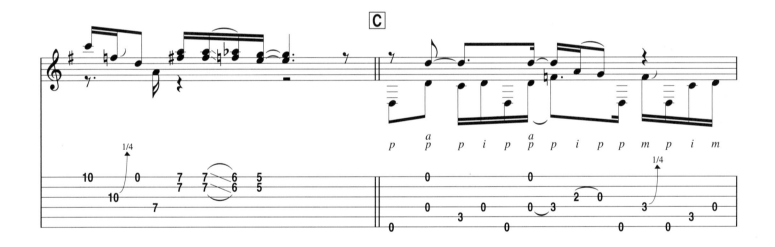

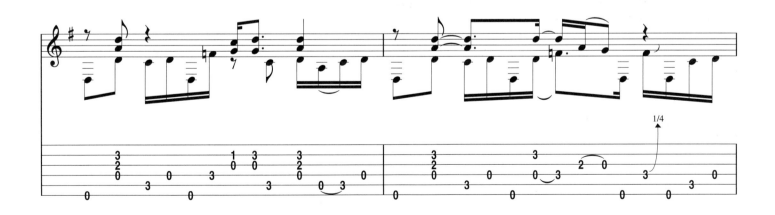

95

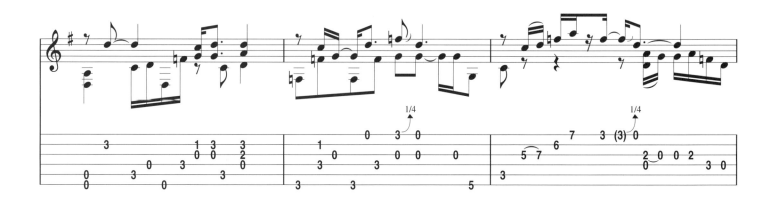

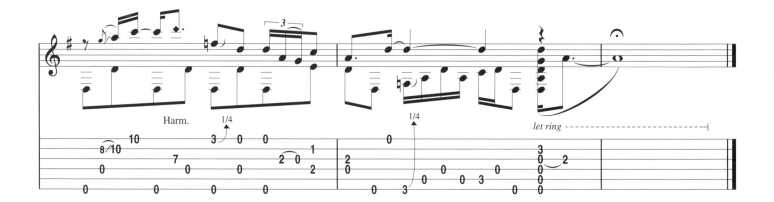

"ANJI"

DAVY GRAHAM

"Anji" is a tune written by Davy Graham, the extremely talented British guitarist who played a large part in the folk revival in England. The tune appeared on his first album (*The Guitar Player*, 1963), but here we'll look at the more famous Paul Simon version, which appeared on *Sounds of Silence* from 1966. The year before recording *Sounds of Silence*, Paul had spent a year in England, where he had no doubt been influenced by Graham and initially inspired to cover the song.

The tune is fairly repetitive and largely based off a i–♭VII–♭VI–V progression, which, in the key of A minor, is fingered as Am–G–F–E. However, a capo placed on the second fret causes the song to sound in the key of Bm. This tune is an ideal one with which to practice your right hand independence, as it largely consists of a palm-muted bass line played by the thumb (or thumbpick) with a decorated melody above played by the fingers. Pay special attention to these other elements too, though:

- Paul makes use of many bends throughout (both whole-step and half-step), which lend a bluesy quality to the proceedings.

- Throughout the song, bass notes are struck while melody notes are being hammered on, bent and released, or pulled off. If you haven't mastered these independence techniques yet, you'll be forced to here!

- Paul uses 6th intervals to play melodies, which helps to break up the monotony of the repetitive progression. This is a technique he made use of in several other fingerstyle songs, most notably "Bookends Theme" from the classic *Bookends* album.

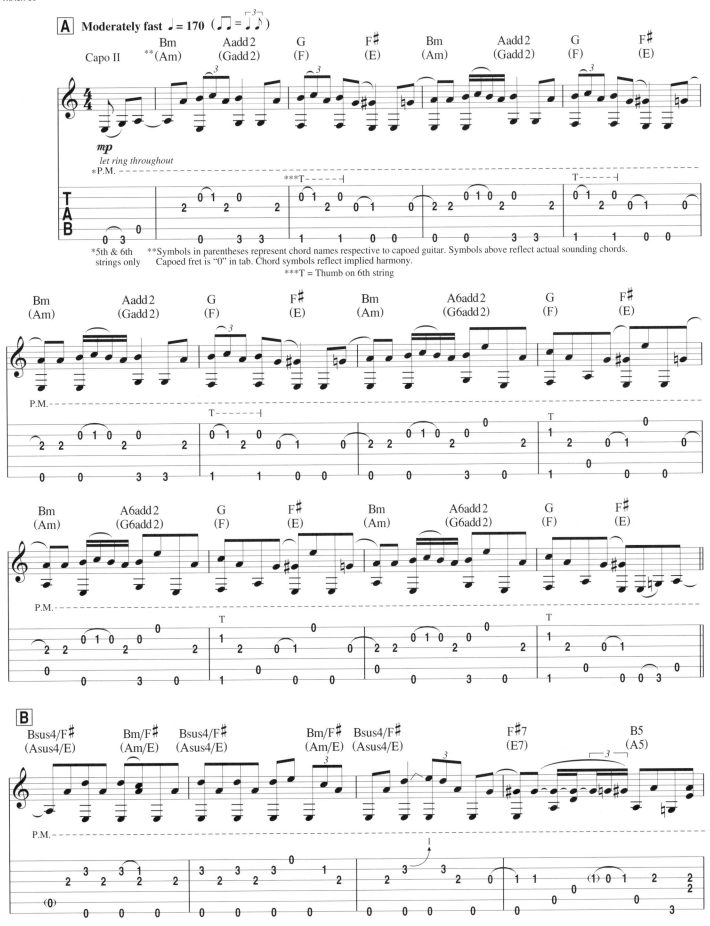

Words and Music by DAVY GRAHAM
© 1965 (Renewed 1993) EMI ROBBINS MUSIC LTD.
All Rights in the U.S. and Canada Controlled and Administered by GLENWOOD MUSIC CORP.

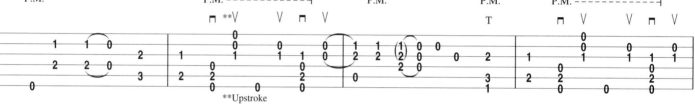

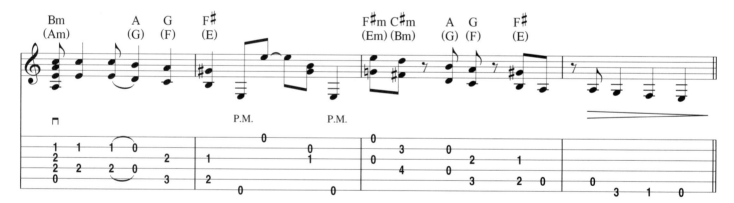

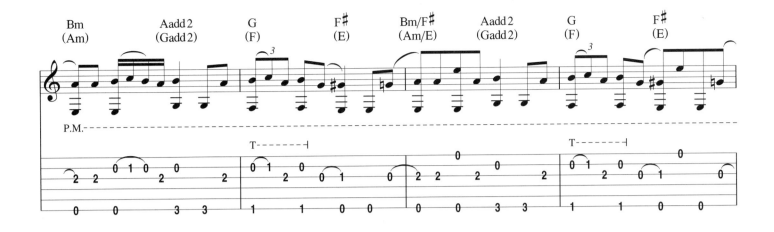

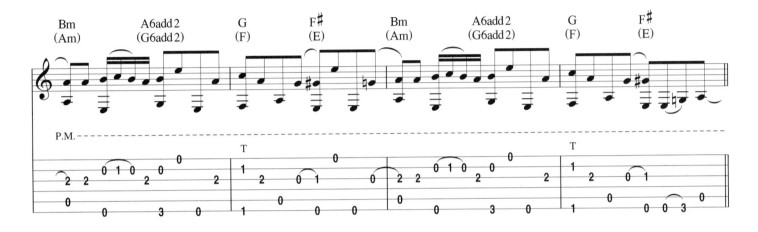

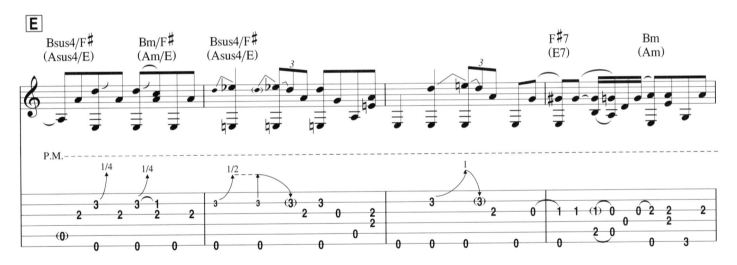

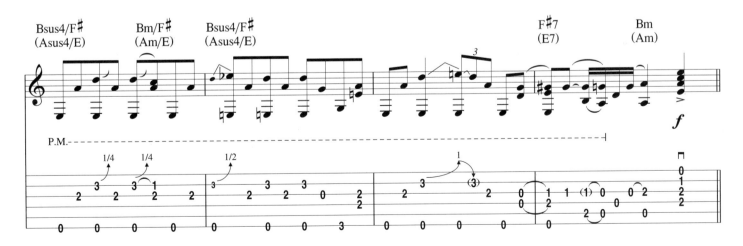

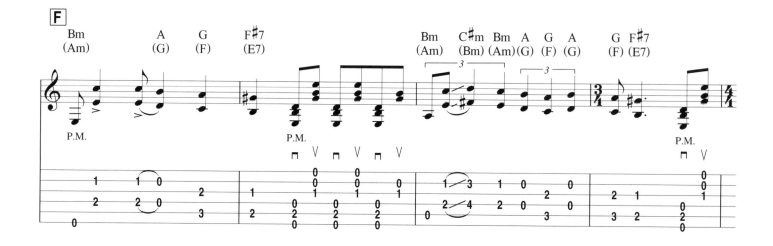

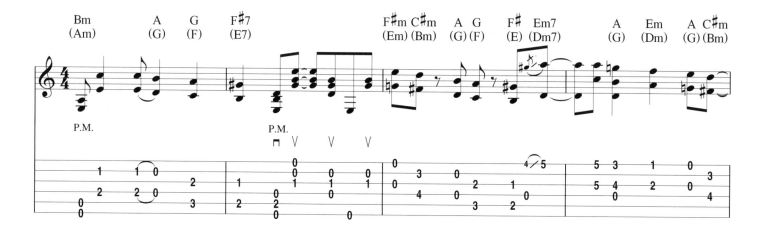

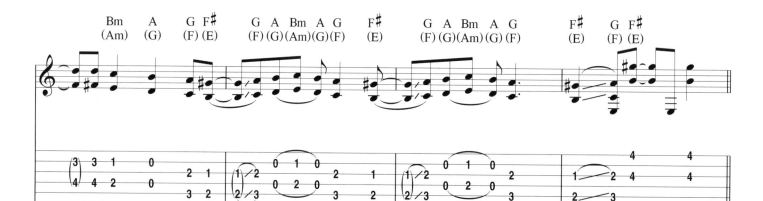

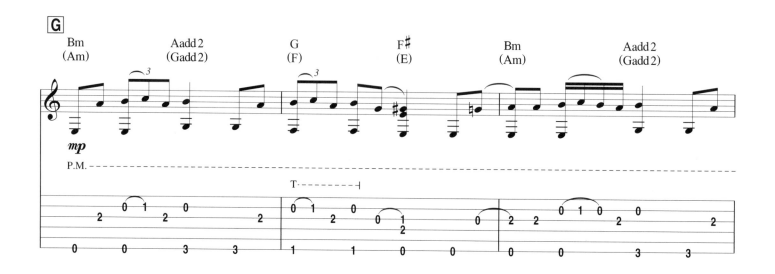

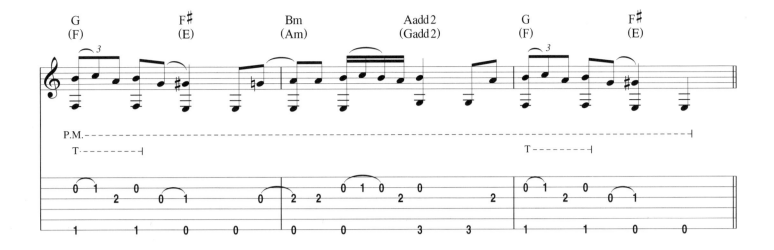

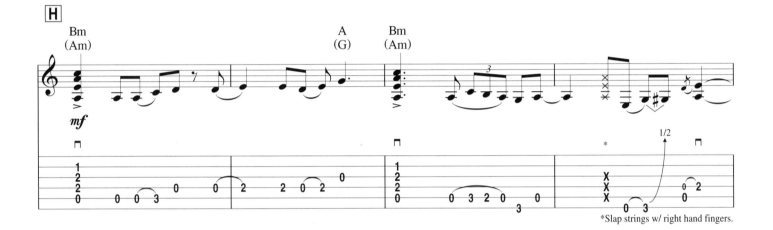

*Slap strings w/ right hand fingers.

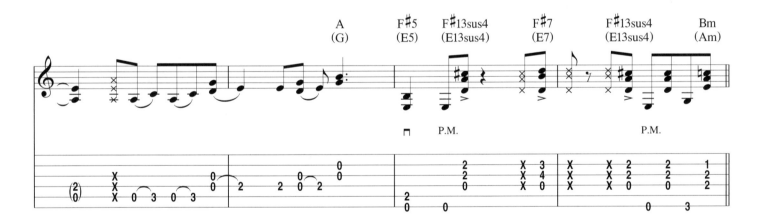

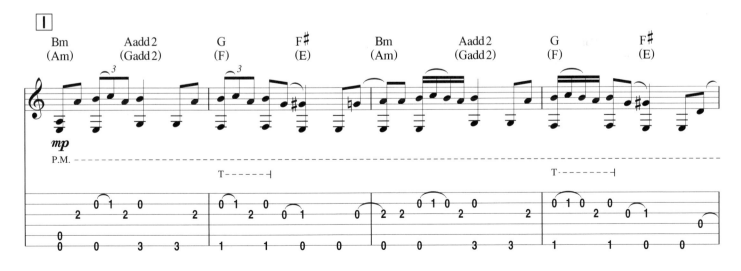

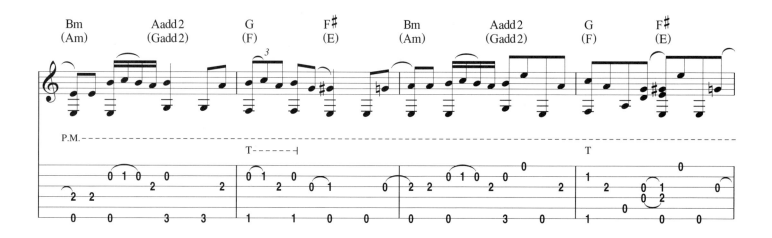

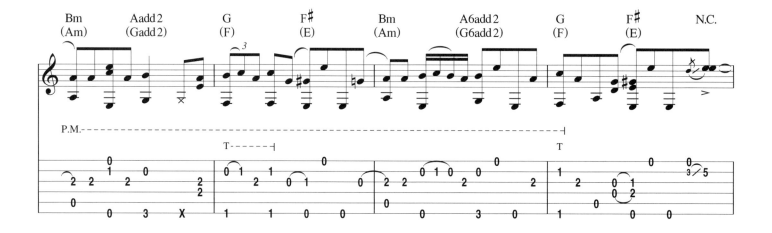

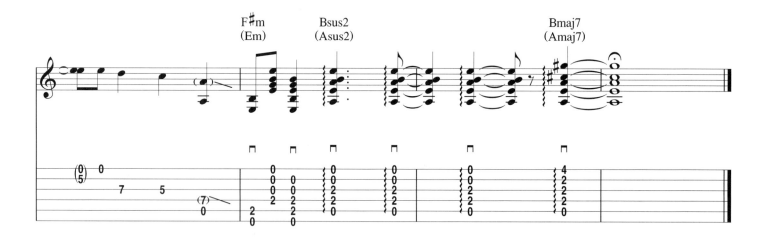

AFTERWORD

Well, that does it for the *Hal Leonard Fingerstyle Guitar Method*. Hopefully you've attained a solid grasp on several usable and essential fingerstyle techniques as well as an understanding of when and how to apply them. As you progress in your fingerstyle studies, seek out the recordings of great fingerstyle guitarists, like the ones mentioned in this book. Listen with an analytical ear to their melodies, bass lines, phrasing styles, and ornamental techniques, and then incorporate those elements into your own style. If you keep an open mind and remember that there's always something new you can learn, you will achieve your fingerstyle goals. But most importantly, have fun. That, after all, is what making music is all about. Good luck!

HAL LEONARD GUITAR METHOD **BOOK 1**

SECOND EDITION

CD INCLUDED

BY WILL SCHMID AND GREG KOCH

HAL LEONARD GUITAR METHOD

THE HAL LEONARD GUITAR METHOD is designed for anyone just learning to play acoustic or electric guitar. It is based on years of teaching guitar students of all ages, and it also reflects some of the best guitar teaching ideas from around the world. This comprehensive method includes: A learning sequence carefully paced with clear instructions; popular songs which increase the incentive to learn to play; versatility – can be used as self-instruction or with a teacher; audio accompaniments so that students have fun and sound great while practicing.

BOOK 1

Book 1 provides beginning instruction which includes tuning, playing position, musical symbols, notes in first position, the C, G, G7, D, D7, A7, and Em chords, rhythms through eighth notes, strumming and picking, 100 great songs, riffs, and examples. Includes a chord chart and well-known songs: Ode to Joy • Rockin' Robin • Greensleeves • Give My Regards to Broadway • Time Is on My Side.

00699010 Book $6.99
00699027 Book/CD Pack $10.95

BOOK 2

INCLUDES TAB

Book 2 continues the instruction started in Book 1 and covers: Am, Dm, A, E, F and B7 chords; power chords; finger-style guitar; syncopations, dotted rhythms, and triplets; Carter style solos; bass runs; pentatonic scales; improvising; tablature; 92 great songs, riffs and examples; notes in first and second position; and more! The CD includes 57 full-band tracks.

00699020 Book $6.99
00697313 Book/CD Pack $9.95

BOOK 3

INCLUDES TAB

Book 3 covers: the major, minor, pentatonic, and chromatic scales, sixteenth notes; barre chords; drop D tuning; movable scales; notes in fifth position; slides, hammer-ons, pull-offs, and string bends; chord construction; gear; 90 great songs, riffs, and examples; and more! The CD includes 61 full-band tracks.

00699030 Book $6.95
00697316 Book/CD Pack $9.95

COMPOSITE

Books 1, 2, and 3 bound together in an easy-to-use spiral binding.
00699040 Books Only $14.95
00697342 Book/3-CD Pack $22.95

VIDEO AND DVD

FOR THE BEGINNING ELECTRIC OR ACOUSTIC GUITARIST

DVD VIDEO | VHS | INCLUDES TAB

00697318 DVD $19.95
00320159 VHS Video $14.95
00697341 Book/CD Pack and DVD $24.95

SONGBOOKS

EASY POP RHYTHMS
00697336 Book $6.95
00697309 Book/CD Pack $14.95

MORE EASY POP RHYTHMS
00697338 Book $6.95
00697322 Book/CD Pack............................$14.95

EVEN MORE EASY POP RHYTHMS
00697340 Book $6.95
00697323 Book/CD Pack............................$14.95

EASY POP MELODIES
Play along with your favorite hits from the Beatles, Elton John, Elvis Presley, the Police, Nirvana, and more!
00697281 Book $6.95
00697268 Book/CD Pack............................$14.95

MORE EASY POP MELODIES
00697280 Book $6.95
00697269 Book/CD Pack............................$14.95

EVEN MORE EASY POP MELODIES
00699154 Book $6.95
00697270 Book/CD Pack............................$14.95

LEAD LICKS
Over 200 licks in all styles.
00697345 Book/CD Pack............................$9.95

RHYTHM RIFFS
Over 200 riffs in all styles.
00697346 Book/CD Pack............................$9.95

STYLISTIC METHODS

ACOUSTIC GUITAR
by Chad Johnson
INCLUDES TAB

00697347 Book/CD Pack....................................$16.95

BLUES GUITAR
by Greg Koch
INCLUDES TAB
00697326 Book/CD Pack....................................$16.95

CHRISTIAN GUITAR
by Chad Johnson
INCLUDES TAB
00695947 Book/CD Pack....................................$12.95

CLASSICAL GUITAR
by Paul Henry
00697376 Book/CD Pack....................................$14.95

COUNTRY GUITAR
by Greg Koch
INCLUDES TAB
00697337 Book/CD Pack....................................$22.99

FINGERSTYLE GUITAR
by Chad Johnson
INCLUDES TAB
00697378 Book/CD Pack....................................$14.95

FLAMENCO GUITAR
by Hugh Burns
INCLUDES TAB
00697363 Book/CD Pack....................................$14.99

JAZZ GUITAR
by Jeff Schroedl
INCLUDES TAB
00695359 Book/CD Pack....................................$19.95

ROCK GUITAR
by Michael Mueller
INCLUDES TAB
00697319 Book/CD Pack....................................$16.95

R&B GUITAR
by Dave Rubin
INCLUDES TAB
00697356 Book/CD Pack....................................$14.95

REFERENCE

ARPEGGIO FINDER
AN EASY-TO-USE GUIDE TO OVER 1,300 GUITAR ARPEGGIOS
00697352 6" x 9" Edition $5.99
00697351 9" x 12" Edition $6.99

INCREDIBLE CHORD FINDER
AN EASY-TO-USE GUIDE TO OVER 1,100 GUITAR CHORDS
00697200 6" x 9" Edition $5.99
00697208 9" x 12" Edition $6.99

INCREDIBLE SCALE FINDER
AN EASY-TO-USE GUIDE TO OVER 1,300 GUITAR SCALES
00695568 6" x 9" Edition $5.99
00695490 9" x 12" Edition $6.99

PAPERBACK LESSONS – HAL LEONARD GUITAR METHOD
by Will Schmid and Greg Koch
All three volumes of the world-famous Hal Leonard Guitar Method are now available in one convenient paperback-sized edition, 4-1/4" x 6-3/4"!
00240326 ....$7.95

Prices, contents and availability subject to change without notice.

FOR MORE INFORMATION, SEE YOUR LOCAL MUSIC DEALER, OR WRITE TO:

HAL • LEONARD® CORPORATION
7777 W. BLUEMOUND RD. P.O. BOX 13819 MILWAUKEE, WI 53213

31901055364980

www.halleonard.com

0609